VESSELS

USEFUL TO THE LORD

WITNESS LEE

Living Stream Ministry
Anaheim, California • www.lsm.org

© 2003 Living Stream Ministry

First Edition, January 2003.

ISBN 0-7363-2207-8

Published by

Living Stream Ministry
2431 W. La Palma Ave., Anaheim, CA 92801 U.S.A.
P. O. Box 2121, Anaheim, CA 92814 U.S.A.

Printed in the United States of America

03 04 05 06 07 08 09 / 9 8 7 6 5 4 3 2 1

CONTENTS

PREFACE

This book is a translation of messages given in Chinese by Brother Witness Lee in the Full-Time Training in Taipei, Taiwan from October through December of 1985. These messages were not reviewed by the speaker.

CHAPTER ONE

THE PURSUIT AND LEARNING OF THE TRUTH

Before we get into the subject matter of this message, I would like to fellowship with you concerning hymns. For the upcoming gospel campaign I have written a new hymn entitled, "The Mystery of the Universe."

1 The heavens God's glory declare,
   And the sky the work of His hands.
   From day to night, to all the earth,
   The things of God they speak forth.
   God's eternal power and attributes
   Though invisible to human eyes,
   Through creation they are made manifest,
   By things made are realized.

2 The living God who made all things
   Did not leave Himself without witness,
   In doing good by filling
   Our hearts with food and gladness.
   The true, eternal God blesses us
   With rain from heav'n and crops from earth.
   The God who grants to us earthly wealth—
   Remember and praise bring forth.

3 The Lord who is God of all things
   To all men gives life and breath.
   He sets their seasons and boundaries
   That they might seek and grope for Him.
   Our God is hidden, invisible,
   The secret of the universe,
   The meaning of the universe—
   All men should discern this truth.

4 Th' invisible God, man could see
   In creation, yet not completely.
   God's person and His image
   Through man expressed had yet to be.
   So Jesus Christ, God's Beloved, came
   To the world in human likeness.
   Through Him completely expressed was God—
   His nature and all He is.

5 Mysterious Christ, Savior mine,
   Manifested God among men.
   God infinite, in eternity,
   Yet man in time, finite to be;
   O Christ, who is God's embodiment,
   God is mingled with man—what good news!
   As God yet man, He would enter us
   To be our portion blessed.

6 God's nature was hidden in Him;
   God's image, expressed through Him.
   In flesh He hast redemption wrought;
   As Spirit, oneness with me sought.
   Christ was incarnated as the God-man
   To redeem us by His shed blood.
   In resurrection as Spirit He
   Comes into us as our life.

This hymn was written according to the fundamental truths in the Scriptures. The first stanza is based on Psalm 19 and Romans 1, which tell us that heaven, earth, and all things reveal God in His eternal power and the outward manifestation of His divine characteristics. Romans 1:20 uses the term *divine characteristics*, which is a translation of the Greek word *theiotes*. A similar Greek word, *theotetos*, is used in Colossians 2:9. This word is translated *Godhead* and refers to God's person or God's divinity. Both *theiotes* and *theotetos* are derived from the Greek word *theos*, which means "God." God's divine characteristics are His distinctive features, whereas His divinity is His very nature. For example, the oak trees of Texas have a distinctive grain. This is one of their characteristics. In addition to this characteristic, they also have the distinct nature of wood. The nature is something inward; the characteristics are an outward manifestation. Whereas God's divinity, His very nature, is what God is, His divine characteristics are the outward manifestation of His nature. Heaven, earth, and all things manifest God's divine characteristics, but they do not express God's person, nature, or image. God Himself is expressed only through man.

The Bible shows us that before the Lord became a man, the heavens, the earth, and all things manifested God's divine characteristics. When the Lord Jesus came to be a man, He not only manifested God's divine characteristics and power but also expressed God's person and image, that is, God's divinity. Romans 1:20 does not speak of God Himself but of God's manifested characteristics. God is love, light, holiness, and righteousness. These are some of the divine characteristics seen in God's creation. Everything created by God is beautiful and lovely, bright and good, orderly and proper. Hence, God's creation manifests God's characteristics. The Lord Jesus, however, was the expression not only of God's characteristics but of God Himself. According to Colossians 2:9, all the fullness of the Godhead, the deity, was expressed in the Lord Jesus bodily.

The second and third stanzas of this hymn are based on the gospel messages that Paul gave in Acts 14 and 17 respectively. The essence of his message in Acts 14 is that God sends us rain from heaven and gives us fruitful seasons, filling our hearts with food and gladness (vv. 15-17). This is a relatively shallow gospel. In Acts 17 Paul spoke in a deeper and more logical way, saying that God made the world and all things and gives life and breath to all people. Paul also pointed out that God determined beforehand the appointed seasons and boundaries of the nations "that they might seek God, if perhaps they might grope for Him and find Him" (vv. 24-27). This implies that God is a God who hides Himself (Isa. 45:15) and that He is a mystery to the human race. In other words, the invisible God is the mystery of the universe (Col. 1:15). Only when we know and receive God, can we understand the mystery of the universe.

There are many fundamental truths revealed in the New Testament. First, God is invisible; He is a God who hides Himself. Second, heaven, earth, and all things reveal God's divine characteristics. Third, the Lord Jesus Himself lived out the person, image, being, and divinity of the invisible God, the God who hides Himself. Therefore, stanza 4 of this hymn says, "Th' invisible God man could see / In creation, yet not completely. / God's person and His image / Through man expressed had yet to be." This means that although the invisible God was manifested through the things that He created, this revelation was still incomplete because a man was needed to express God's person and image. This man was the Lord Jesus. Hence, the following lines say, "So Jesus Christ, God's Beloved, came / To the world in human likeness. / Through Him completely expressed was God— / His nature and all He is."

The first stanza of this hymn concerns the divine characteristics, and the fourth stanza concerns the divine nature. The divine characteristics were manifested through creation, but the divine nature was expressed through the Lord Jesus. This divine nature, which refers to what God is, was expressed to the uttermost through the Lord Jesus. Therefore, the last two stanzas, which offer praise to the Lord Jesus, turn from God's creation to the Lord Jesus. Stanza 5 says, "Mysterious Christ, Savior mine, / Manifested God among men. / God infinite, in eternity, / Yet man in time, finite to be; / O Christ, who is God's embodiment, / God is mingled with man—what good news! / As God yet man, He would enter us / To be our portion blessed." As the mysterious and wonderful One, the Lord Jesus is the infinite God who became a finite man. Hence, He is truly God and truly man; He is God mingled with man. This One is the good news of great joy, the wonderful, glad tidings. Moreover, as such a One He wants to come into us to be our blessed portion.

Stanza 6 says, "God's nature was hidden in Him; / God's image, expressed through Him. / In flesh He hast redemption wrought; / As Spirit, oneness with me sought. / Christ was incarnated as the God-man / To redeem us by His shed blood. / In resurrection as Spirit He / Comes into us as our life." The

Lord Jesus accomplished redemption so that He could enter into us to be our life. The fifth stanza speaks about our blessed portion, and the sixth stanza speaks about life.

This is an excellent gospel hymn because it uses various terms and phrases of the truth, such as *God is hidden, invisible, mysterious Christ, Savior, God's embodiment, the God-man,* and *incarnated.* All of these terms are rich and deep in meaning and help explain the truth of the gospel in a concise way. This hymn tells us that the Lord Jesus was put to death on the cross, shedding His precious blood to redeem us, the sinners, and that He was resurrected to become the life-giving Spirit so that in our experience He could come into our spirit to be our life. Hence, this short hymn of six stanzas begins with God's creation and concludes with the Lord as God's embodiment coming into us to be one with us in our spirit as our life. This hymn comprises nearly all of the crucial truths in the Scriptures.

The deepest thought in this hymn is that the Lord Jesus was God mingled with man. This was God's aspiration from eternity before the times of the ages. His desire was that He would create man and enter into man, not only to be united with man but also to be mingled with man. This aspiration was fulfilled when He was incarnated and became a man. The Lord Jesus was God mingled with man. Furthermore, this One came into us so that, like Him, we would also become those who are the mingling of God with man. This is the content of the gospel and the wonderful, good news.

THE IMPORTANCE OF HYMNS

Among us we need some who not only know the truth but who can also compose and sing hymns. If we desire to work for the Lord, we need to study and speak the Lord's word. To speak for the Lord, we must first know the Lord's word; that is, we must know the truth. Next, our spirit must be a strong, praying spirit, and we need to practice praying unceasingly. Third, we must develop our speaking ability. Fourth, we must also be able to sing. Both Ephesians 5 and Colossians 3 tell us that God's word is not only for us to speak to others but also for us to sing to others (Eph. 5:19; Col. 3:16). In the past singing has been our weakest area. I hope that from now on singing would be more prevailing both in the small group meetings and in the big meetings.

Of course, some are born without a talent for singing. However, in our singing we should not focus on how beautiful the music is but on the release of our spirit. There are many of us who can sing well and who have been trained in vocal music. However, when we sing in the meetings, instead of paying too much attention to the music and the sound of others' voices, we should pay attention to life and spirit. The singing of the hymns should be an overflow of life and spirit. If we touch life and spirit in our enjoyment of the Lord, spontaneously we will be filled with singing. Sometimes during a meeting a saint will choose a hymn from the hymnal and ask everyone to sing it in order to fill up the time. This makes our singing regulated and formal. Instead, we should enjoy the Lord to such an extent that we spontaneously overflow with singing. This may have been the way the early saints sang in their meetings. We do not, however, have this kind of situation among us.

The saints' singing of hymns began with David in the Old Testament. The tunes from these hymns were then passed down from David all the way to the Catholic Church and then from the Catholic Church to the Protestant churches. Those who study music know that these "sacred melodies" have a distinct style that is grave and solemn. After World War II the Americans, who like new things, called these sacred tunes the "Old Timers," so they discarded them and composed many new tunes. Most of the new tunes, however, did not stand the test of time because they were not dignified enough. Hence, most of them are of little value. Nevertheless, we selected some of the new tunes that have some value and included them in our hymnal. One example is the tune to the hymn "In the Garden." The content of this hymn is a description of how Mary the Magdalene met the Lord Jesus in the garden on the morning of His resurrection and how the two of them conversed and fellowshipped with one another. Over twenty years ago when I heard the tune of this hymn, I used it to compose *Hymns,* #501, "O Glorious Christ, Savior Mine."

This is also the tune that we have used for the newly written gospel hymn. It is a dignified, sacred tune. Another hymn that uses one of the new tunes is *Hymns,* #608, "What Mystery, the Father, Son, and Spirit." The tune of this hymn is also very dignified. All good hymns have solemn tunes.

In this gospel campaign we will also use *Hymns,* #987, which is an excellent gospel hymn written by the American evangelist J. Wilbur Chapman. In Chapman's days, the prevailing theology was the theology taught by the modernists. The modernists said that the Lord Jesus was not God, that His death had not been for redemption, and that He had not been resurrected. Therefore, Chapman purposely wrote this hymn of five verses. The first verse is on the birth of the Lord Jesus, the second verse is on His death, the third verse is on His burial, the fourth verse is on His resurrection, and the fifth verse is on His coming back. This hymn not only has a dignified tune, but its chorus is also particularly well written, pointing out the subject matter of all five verses. The chorus says, "Living, He loved me; dying, He saved me; / Buried, He carried my sins far away; / Rising, He justified freely forever: / One day He's coming—O glorious day!" The content of this hymn is proper and rich, and the tune is dignified.

THE LEARNING NECESSARY
FOR WRITING HYMNS

We all know that poetry is the crystallization or the cream of literature. A person who is able to produce poetry in various forms has reached the peak of his literary training. Furthermore, poetry is also based upon the experience of human life. It is the product of the expression of human sentiments. Little children cannot write good poetry because they lack the experiences of human life. To learn how to write hymns, we need three things—the knowledge of the truth, the experience of life, and some attainment in literature. It is not necessary for us to be highly educated in literature, but we should at least have a certain measure of literary attainment. By also having the knowledge of the truth and the experience of life, we will be able to write good hymns.

A NEW HYMN—"THE MEANING OF HUMAN LIFE"

Another new hymn for this gospel campaign is "The Meaning of Human Life":

1   God made man a vessel he
     With a spirit, soul, body.
     God to man his content be
     That through man His glory see.

2   Man does have God's image true,
     Noble in his status, too.
     But God's life man also needs
     Divine nature to receive.

3   Christ in death as God expressed
     Man redeemed, His blood was shedd'st.
     In His resurrection He
     Enters us our life to be.

4   Man without Christ will perceive
     That all things are vanity.
     Human life is meaningless
     Without hope or purpose.

5   But when man takes Christ as life,
     He's in spirit born anew.
     When he daily lives by Christ,
     Vanity is turned to song.

6   Therefore, man can God express
     That the whole world he would bless.
     Living water flowing out
     People's thirst to satisfy.

7   When in glory Christ returns
     Glorified our body be
     To His glorious body conformed
     With Him for eternity.

In order to know a hymn, we first need to learn to pay attention to its special features. Sometimes only a few lines or stanzas of a hymn are good, or perhaps only a certain part is outstanding. For example, the hymn "The Meaning of

Human Life" has seven stanzas, but stanzas 4 and 5 are the best. Stanza 4 speaks about man's sense of vanity and emptiness, and stanza 5 speaks about man's experience of joy and satisfaction. When we preach about the meaning of human life, we need to speak about man's sense of vanity and emptiness on the negative side and man's experience of joy and satisfaction on the positive side.

Stanza 4 is the peak of this hymn on the negative side. It does not merely say that all things are vanity. Rather, it says that man perceives that all things are vanity. Vanity is not a doctrine or a theory that convinces people in their mind. Vanity is a feeling of human life and the conclusion of human experience. Furthermore, this stanza repeatedly uses the word *without* to intensify the feeling of vanity. On the other hand, stanza 5 is the climax of this hymn on the positive side, describing the human life of vanity being turned into song. When the human life is full of joyful singing, it is full of song. These two stanzas comprise a complete gospel message.

THE RELATIONSHIP BETWEEN SERVICE AND TRUTH

In this message my main purpose is not to teach you to learn the hymns but to fellowship with you a burden regarding your pursuit and learning. Those of you who are presently serving full time have the day off on Monday, are working on the campuses on Saturday, and are attending meetings on the Lord's Day. Therefore, this leaves only four days a week for studying. In the beginning I had hoped that every full-timer would have half a day every day to study the New Testament, including the Recovery Version and the life-study messages.

The most important thing that we who have given ourselves to work for the Lord can do is to speak for Him. Whether we are preaching the gospel, teaching the truth, ministering life, exhorting the believers, or building the church, we need to speak for the Lord. Hence, it is very important for a person who works for the Lord to study the word.

In 1949 I began the work in Taiwan, and in 1952 I began to conduct trainings. I did this every year for ten years until 1961. Every year there was a great number of saints who attended the training. The highest and best training was the one held in 1953. I am full of thanksgiving to the Lord for the saints who were in that term of the training because they have a strong desire for the Lord and have been used by the Lord. Nevertheless, I still feel that there is some lack because they have not adequately entered into the truth. As far as the truth is concerned, they are much better than the workers in Christianity, but they are still not as advanced as the earlier generations of co-workers among us who were thoroughly trained and perfected in the truth.

Every kind of work will be judged by its fruit. The Lord Jesus said that every good tree produces good fruit and that a tree is proven by the fruit it produces (Matt. 7:17-20). More than thirty years have passed since the training began, and now we can see the fruit of the labor of these co-workers. Generally speaking, the results of their labor are quite good. We all know that the Christian group with the longest history on the island of Taiwan is the Presbyterian Church from Scotland, which has been in Taiwan for almost two hundred years. According to the statistics I obtained three years ago, the Presbyterian Church has a little over eighty thousand members. This is the issue of their labor on this island after almost two hundred years. We in the local churches rank second in terms of numbers with over forty thousand members. However, if we were to count the number of people baptized in the local churches as the Presbyterian Church does, we would have about the same number as they do. This indicates that our work in Taiwan during the last thirty years has been comparable to the work of the Presbyterian Church. Not only so, many Western missionaries have admitted in their reports that the most successful evangelistic work in Taiwan has been the work carried out by the Lord's recovery.

I am telling you all these facts to prove that I am not invalidating the work of our co-workers during the last thirty years. Nevertheless, there is a saying, "A boat sailing against the current must forge ahead or else it will be driven back." Therefore, whatever we do, we must always try our best and endeavor to improve. Concerning this matter, this particular group of co-workers, who are a generation younger than I and whom I almost single-handedly trained by myself, has been a disappointment to me. They accomplished only a certain amount in the last thirty years and did not do more. They stopped and did not seek to improve.

In a sense, the work on the island of Taiwan has not gained much profit or made much progress during the ten years from 1975 to 1985. We have merely been maintaining the status quo. By the Lord's grace the co-workers have not brought the churches into disgrace or decline, but neither have they made much progress. The reason for their lack of advancement is that the co-workers are behind in learning the truth. I am disappointed with them because of their lack of aggressiveness. It is never too late for us to learn, because there is no limit to knowledge. The less educated a person is, the less he thinks he needs to learn. Rather, he thinks that what he has learned is adequate and acceptable. The more educated a person is, however, the more he feels that he is inadequate and needs to learn more aggressively.

THE CHANGE OF SYSTEM
NEEDING TO BE MATCHED BY THE WORD

The result of my fellowship with the elders is that I have seen a very clear picture. The church in Taipei has over ten thousand saints, and over three thousand of them regularly attend meetings in the twenty-one halls in Taipei. However, the ministry of the word in each hall is very weak. Therefore, there has not been any spreading in our work. Ever since we changed the system in October, many other churches have had a great increase. The churches in Yungho, Hsinchu, Taichung, Tainan, and Kaohsiung have had increases of over fifty percent. The church in Taipei is the only exception. Not only has there been no increase in Taipei, but the number of saints has actually decreased by five percent.

When we first began to change the system, I made a statement saying that our practice was in the initial stage. We were like those doing research in a laboratory, trying to find a new way that was according to the Scriptures. Therefore, we appointed the leading deacons in every hall as elders in order to let them try to lead the church. Now, after looking at the results of our experiment during the past one and a half years, the elders and I have found that our numbers have decreased instead of increased. This shows us that there is a weakness here.

The church in Taipei is a church that has great assets and is rich in resources. When I began the work here on August 1, 1949, the number of regular attendants in Taipei was less than one hundred. Five months later at the end of that year, the number of attendants in Taipei had increased to nine hundred. After five more years the number of saints on the entire island had increased a hundred times. The number on the whole island when we first began the work was around four to five hundred, but in 1955, prior to Brother Austin-Sparks' visit, we had forty to fifty thousand people according to our estimation. In other words, there was a hundredfold increase in less than six years. This was the rate of increase during the initial stage of our work in Taiwan. Now we have a great asset of three to four thousand saints in Taipei, yet after ten months of implementing the change of system, we have not brought in even a thousand. This indicates that there is a big weakness among us.

I came back to seriously and thoroughly study our situation to find out the reason for our low rate of increase. Although I was not able to visit every hall or contact every elder, after a detailed analysis I concluded that the main reason for our low rate of increase is the weakness in our ministering of the word. We must realize that people come to the meetings not because the meeting hall is nice, because the people are nice, or because of other factors. The only reason they come is because of the strong ministry of the word and the transmission of the rich truths. The reason the church in Yungho has had a great increase is that the leading brother studies the Word with the full-timers so that they are strengthened to speak the truth. This attracts people.

MAN BEING CREATED WITH AN INNATE ABILITY
TO LOVE THE TRUTH

Man has an innate ability to love the truth. There are clear indications of this in the Bible. When the Lord Jesus began His ministry, He mostly preached the word on the mountains and in the wilderness. There were no luxurious or comfortable facilities, yet people came in flocks. When John Wesley was raised up in England, he preached on the streets. One of Wesley's contemporaries, George Whitefield, who was considered to be more powerful than him, preached in the open fields. In those days there were no microphones or proper facilities. The preachers simply raised their voices and spoke loudly, and people went in crowds to listen to them. Today our speaking is weak. We cannot compensate for this weakness with money, knowledge, or capability. People do not want our knowledge, eloquence, or capability. Rather, they desire the supplying word. This innate ability to love the truth was created by God.

When God created man, He put in man a longing to seek after knowledge. This is why people have a desire to know about the things around them from their youth. A wise mother will not force her children to do things or punish them by beating them when she teaches them. Rather, she will speak to them a great deal, and by her speaking, she will transfuse knowledge into them. The Westerners are not necessarily better than the Chinese in educating their children, but one good point about the Westerners is that they often read a story to their children at bedtime. Furthermore, sometimes when a mother finds that her little boy is being naughty, instead of spanking him, she will read him a story. Once the boy begins to listen to the story, he calms down, behaves properly, becomes obedient, and stops being naughty. This is because within him there is a desire to obtain more knowledge. The more a child learns, the more he is happy and satisfied.

SETTING OUR HEART TO LEARN THE TRUTH

During my stay this time I have observed that the churches everywhere are lacking in the ministry of the word, not only in the big meetings but even more so in the small meetings. In a sense, our meetings abound in every aspect except the ministry of the word. This is a great shortage. If I had stayed here for a year, I would not have let this matter go lightly. The truths and the riches among us are all being stored in the bookroom with no effect. This is a very regrettable matter.

The co-workers who received my training thirty years ago and who were trained for as long as ten years have done quite a good job during all these years. On the other hand, however, their ministry of the word has been merely average. The truths and the riches given to us by the Lord have all been released, but they have been put on the shelves and are not being used. Perhaps you may say, "Oh, we use them. We are all using them." According to my consideration, however, using them improperly is equivalent to not using them. This is similar to someone having a ball but not knowing how to use it to play a game. This is a big problem.

This is the reason I encouraged hundreds of you to rise up and serve full time. You have responded, and the churches are willing to cooperate. What I am afraid of the most, however, is that you will fall into the same trap. Therefore, I hope that you can complete at least one course of the training in the Lord's word. This does not mean that when you graduate, your brain will be filled with knowledge. Rather, it means that you will know how to use the Lord's word, how to study the truth, and how to preach the word. This should not be too difficult for you since you are all at least college graduates. It all depends on whether or not you set your heart on this matter.

Nothing is too difficult for someone who sets his heart to do it. There is nothing that you cannot do; it all depends upon whether or not you put your heart into it. If you put your heart into something, you can do it. This is what we mean when we say, "Where there is a will, there is a way." The problem is that by nature man loves ease and hates work. Laziness is second nature to man. I am very concerned about this matter. I have a considerable amount of human experience, and I realize that all humans tend to be easygoing. However, you should not be loose in any way during your first five years of full-time service because these are the most crucial years of your service. You must lay hold of these five years. What matters is not what you do but how much you learn. The most important thing is to learn the truth and the experiences of life. You need to try to advance as quickly as possible in these two matters.

For your sake I would use myself as an example. When I began corresponding with Brother Watchman Nee in 1925, I mostly asked him questions concerning the Scriptures. It was not until 1932, when I invited him to speak in my hometown of Chefoo, that I met him for the first time. As a result of his visit, a church was raised up in Chefoo in July of the same year. Through the Lord's blessing, the number of saints meeting in the church exceeded a hundred. I had to give a message five times a week. This forced me to drop my job and serve full time. Afterward I went to Shanghai to see Brother Nee, and later he asked me to move to Shanghai with my whole family. From then on I became his co-worker. Two years later in October of 1935, Brother Nee held a conference in Kulangsu, Amoy, which is in the province of Fukien, but I did not go with him then. Fifteen years later in 1950, I went to the Philippines. One of the responsible brothers there who had attended the conference in Kulangsu told me that in that conference Brother Nee had told a group of seeking saints, "We have a brother, Witness Lee, whose progress in the truth and in life can be likened not just to running but to flying." Actually, at that time I had not been satisfied with my condition.

Although those of you who are serving full time have already graduated from college, you are still under thirty years of age. Your prospects for the years ahead are bright, and you still have much potential to advance. Therefore, you must treasure this period of time and endeavor to enter into the truth and to learn the experiences in life. What is important now is not how much you read every day but how much you learn and enter into the truth. You can never finish studying the Bible. I have been studying the Bible for sixty and a half years, and the more I study, the more I receive, and the more I sense that there is more to study. If time allows, I would like to have another life-study of the Bible that would be different from what we had in the past. Our study of the truths in the Bible will never end.

FIGHTING THE GOOD FIGHT FOR THE TRUTH

In the United States over one hundred churches with over ten thousand saints have been raised up since the Lord's recovery began there. Although the number is small, those who oppose us as well as those who agree with us admit that we are above everyone else regarding the truth. Many of you know that we won the lawsuits related to the two books called *The God-Men* and *The Mindbenders*. The "Statement of Decision" issued by the Superior Court of California in relation to the case against the publisher of *The God-Men* contains thirty-two pages. I hope you get the opportunity to read it so that you may understand why we initiated the lawsuit.

I bring this matter up because it is related to our history. Those who belong to this generation should be clear about this matter. It is all right to argue concerning the truth in America because America is a country of free speech. It is all right for Christians to say that Buddhism is wrong and vice versa. This kind of argument is not in violation of the law. However, if you attack others by intentionally slandering them or by fabricating lies or twisting the facts with an evil intention to hurt others, then you are committing libel, which is a criminal offense according to the law. We took the legal actions not only to fight for the truth but also to clear our name.

The Background

The main target of our litigation was the book called *The Mindbenders*. The author, who wrote the book in 1977, put numerous false statements, false accusations, and slanderous words against us in the book. Moreover, he fabricated cases accusing us of deceiving people. In 1978 after the members of the People's Temple committed mass suicide in Jonestown, Guyana, the author of *The Mindbenders* added another chapter to the book concerning this matter, saying that the situation was far more serious in the "Local Churches." As a result, some of the parents of our younger saints were concerned that their children had joined a deceptive organization. In America there is a profession called "deprogramming." When a physician certifies that a young person is mentally abnormal, the parents can hire people to force their children to be "deprogrammed." There was such a case on the East Coast. A couple hired some people to seize their son, who was studying at a medical school in Texas, for "deprogramming." Fortunately, the people whom they hired did not act foolishly. After some investigation they realized that there was no problem with that young brother, that he was mentally sound, and that the church that he was attending was also very proper. Therefore, they sent him back. There were many more cases like this. Furthermore, the author fabricated lies about us and slandered us to such an extent that we were like poisonous snakes and fierce beasts in people's eyes. The book damaged us to the extent that some of the brothers and sisters experienced hardship at their jobs and were even fired.

After this book was published, we wrote hundreds of letters to the publisher, asking for an opportunity to clarify the situation. The publisher, however, refused to meet with us. They did not take our phone calls and would not discuss the issue with us. We also sent five American brothers to visit five different publishers, asking them, "If Witness Lee were not a Chinese, would you have done this?" They all said that they would not have done such a thing. Therefore, it is obvious that they did this because I am Chinese. They were not against foreigners; rather, they despised and scorned me because I was an elderly Chinese who had come to America to teach the truth.

For three years I did not take any action. Then in April of 1980 I was visiting the churches in Colorado and New Mexico. The co-workers there told me that it would be impossible for our work to spread as long as these two books—*The Mindbenders* and *The God-Men*—existed. They said that whenever we contacted someone, the very next day that person would receive a copy of one of the two books and then would not want to be in contact with us any longer. After some careful consideration, I felt that since we had not been able to obtain a proper response from the publishers, for the sake of the future of the Lord's recovery we could not allow this damaging situation to continue to spread. Therefore, according to Paul's principle of appealing to Caesar in Acts, we filed the lawsuits. We all know that originally Paul had been very reluctant about suing his persecutors. However, he had no choice because otherwise he would have been killed, and there would have been no way for the Lord's word to be completed.

The Example of Paul

Today it is as if we are driving a car on the road, but someone has put some obstacles in the middle of the road to frustrate our progress. Therefore, we must first stop our car and clear the road before we can get into our car and continue to drive on. Paul's way of clearing the road was to appeal to Caesar. He did this not merely to file a complaint but to ask for help, because the Jewish officials were corrupt and unrighteous. Felix had hoped that Paul would give him money and therefore asked for Paul to be sent to him frequently. However, Paul did not give him any money and was therefore imprisoned again for two years (24:26-27). Afterward, Festus came to the province as the successor to Felix. The Jews tried to bribe him, entreating him to send Paul from Caesarea to Jerusalem so that they could set an ambush to do away with him on the way (25:1-3). Festus, wanting to gain favor with the Jews, asked Paul if he would be willing to go up to Jerusalem and be judged there. Realizing Festus's craftiness, Paul said, "I am standing before Caesar's judgment seat, where I ought to be judged....I appeal to Caesar" (vv. 9-11). After conferring with the council, Festus had no choice but to say, "To Caesar you have appealed; to Caesar you shall go" (v. 12). In this way Paul was able to escape the hands of the Jews.

Paul remained in Rome for two whole years before his case was presented to Caesar Nero, who pronounced him not guilty and therefore released him. During his two years of imprisonment in Rome, Paul wrote Ephesians, Philippians, Colossians, and Philemon. Afterward he wrote 1 Timothy, 2 Timothy, Titus, and Hebrews. Most Bible students know that the most profound and mysterious truths are in these eight Epistles. Therefore, if Paul had not appealed to Caesar and had been killed by the Jews on his way to Jerusalem, then the Scriptures would have only included the first six of Paul's Epistles—Romans, 1 and 2 Corinthians, Galatians, and 1 and 2 Thessalonians—which were written in the initial stage of his ministry. If this had happened, there would have been a great lack in the divine truth.

The Lawsuits

Based upon Paul's pattern, we found a way out. Like Paul, we were being greatly persecuted and felt quite helpless, so we had no choice but to "appeal to Caesar." This may be likened to calling the police to save our lives when we are confronted by robbers. We call the police not to file a complaint but to ask them to rescue us, lest the robbers kill us. Therefore, I told the brothers and sisters that we should either do nothing, or we should do something in a thorough way. First of all, we would have to pursue the lawsuits to their end, even if this required us to pour out everything we had financially. Furthermore, we would have to have ten to twenty co-workers who would specifically take care of this matter. They would be the ones who would go out to collect evidence within the limits allowed by the law and in a definite way.

Due to the large number of cases that were being presented in the American law courts, we had to wait five years before the trial could start. The court spent five days to hear the case. We presented all our reasons and evidence before the judge. Our opposing party had no way to deny the evidence, which had been produced mostly during the depositions of both parties and had been made under oath in the presence of the clerk appointed by the court. Eventually, the verdict was pronounced. The judge enumerated in a clear way the violations that our opposing party had committed and decided that we had won the case.

DEFENSE AND CONFIRMATION

During the lawsuit, J. Gordon Melton, a theologian, testified in court on our behalf. Over twenty years ago he published the *Encyclopedia of American Religions,* which has a paragraph concerning us. The comments he makes are quite favorable toward us. While he was planning to publish a revised and enlarged edition, the two slanderous books against us were published. He was a supporter of that organization, but as a scholar, he believes that the goal of a writer should be to make a contribution to society. Hence, he felt that he had to do some research to find out the real story. Therefore, he bought our books and did some personal study. After reading the books, his concepts about us completely changed. Not only did he testify on our behalf in court, but after the "Statement of Decision" was issued by the judge, he also wrote an open letter, informing those in fundamental Christianity in the whole United States that our theology is based upon the orthodox theology of the Brethren Assembly and urging people to accept our beliefs.

We must realize that the highest, most fundamental, and proper theology in Christianity is the Brethren theology. The top two seminaries in the United States today are Dallas Theological Seminary and Moody Theological School in Chicago. The teachings in both schools are based upon the Brethren theology. I truly admire Dr. Melton because he was able to find out by reading my books that our theology is according to the Brethren theology. This is proof that he is indeed a devoted scholar.

My main point is that it will not be an easy matter to spread the Lord's recovery in the United States, Europe, Australia, South America, and Africa. The truths that have been released in the Lord's recovery are not mere repetitions of what others have said. Rather, they are all based upon the pure revelation of the Word. The United States is the top Christian country and is first-class in every aspect. It has a wealth of talent and an abundance of seminaries with many theological professors and people with doctorate degrees. However, what I have been speaking is different from what they usually speak. This is not a small matter. Dr. Melton is a reputable, educated theologian. In the beginning he stood on the ground of an opposer, but after reading our books he turned around completely. From this we can see how pure and unadulterated our study of the truth is.

NEEDING TO PROGRESS IN THE STUDY OF THE TRUTH

Today in the twentieth century everything is improving. Although the earth itself cannot be improved, other things such as the means of transportation on the earth can be improved. Likewise, although the Bible does not change, we can advance in our knowledge and study of the Bible and in our interpretation and application of the truth. The Bible has been in the hands of Christians for almost two thousand years, and the revelation contained in it is progressing as the years go by. Today when we come to study the Bible, if we do not know how to use advanced methods to study it, we will fall behind and become out-of-date.

When we undertake a task, we must not be complacent, sticking to old ways and resisting progress. In America I read a news article saying that the population of Taiwan is equal to one-third of the population of France, yet Taiwan's production output is higher than that of France. The reason for this lies in the success of education in Taiwan. In the last forty years the Taiwanese government's greatest contribution to its people has been the success and spread of education, which uplifts the level of people's intelligence and increases their capability. Hence, Taiwan has been completely transformed into an industrial society. Likewise, today if we desire to work for the Lord, we must raise our level of education. If we do not advance, we will be taken over by others and be eliminated.

I believe that in another two or three years we will have over one thousand full-timers. We must be clear that we cannot be like the outdated preachers in Christianity who study theology a little and learn about the Bible a little and then go out to be preachers with a very limited amount of Bible knowledge. We must strive to get into the depths of the Word. In the Lord's recovery we have already had a very good beginning and have laid a very good foundation, all of which will be a big help to you. You should not think that we have finished the life-study of the entire New Testament and that there is only this much revelation in the Scriptures. No, the life-study of the Bible that we have completed is only the beginning. I have already said that if the Lord gives me another twenty to thirty years, I would like to write another set of studies on the New Testament. This task, however, has to be left for you to do. Nevertheless, I believe that what you presently have is enough to serve as an initiation. What you need now is to enter in and to study more deeply. Then you will be able to meet the need of this age.

Today we can easily attract crowds of students through our gospel preaching on the campuses because the students are quite educated and will readily receive the high gospel according to logic and reasoning. In the villages, however, it may not be that easy to preach the gospel due to the people's shortage of knowledge and lack of understanding. In any case, human beings all have the desire to pursue knowledge. If you study the biblical truths thoroughly and then present them to people, especially to the college students, they will fully appreciate what you say. On the contrary, if you are short of the knowledge of the truth, it will be impossible for you to preach the gospel on the campuses effectively. Hence, you must strive to pursue the truth. If you still do things today in the old way—graduate from high school, study two years of theological school, and then go out to be a preacher—that will not work. That way is an outdated way and cannot meet the need of this age. You must exert some effort to be solidly equipped in the truth. This is my main burden for you.

ATTENDING THE GROUP MEETINGS
AND SPEAKING FOR THE LORD

During the training you should do your best to attend the church meetings, particularly the small group meetings. You should not stay together with your fellow trainees all the time. Rather, you should go to different groups to practice speaking for the Lord. You have already been trained for a year and should be able to speak better and more strongly than the saints who have not been trained. In practicing the change of system those who can speak for the Lord are needed the most. I have attended a few groups, and according to my observation, the greatest lack is the lack of speaking, the lack of those who can speak. You may have also noticed the same thing. Therefore, you should have the burden to go and speak in the small groups. If there are one hundred of you and each one goes to a group every week to speak for the Lord, the situation of the small groups will be dramatically changed. This will be a great help to the building up of the small groups in the church in Taipei.

CHAPTER TWO

LEARNING HOW TO SERVE

THE SUCCESS OF THE CHANGE OF SYSTEM DEPENDING UPON THE MINISTRY OF THE WORD

Regarding the changing of the system, the matter that I feel most heavily burdened about within is the weakness of the ministry of the word in the meetings. At the present time the new way has proven to be the right way both in the East and in the West. However, all the situations and conditions that were manifested during the experimental period have shown us that the speaking of the word in the various meetings is very weak. We are not asking that the speaking be extraordinary but that it would at least be able to meet the need. Presently, our speaking is not ideal and does not meet the need. In other words, we are like a team that cannot take the field to compete because we are not up to the standard.

I have always been heavily burdened concerning the ministry of the word, and I have been forced to carefully consider before the Lord how to deal with it. For example, consider the church in Taipei. It is a large church with over twenty meeting halls and more than four hundred small groups, yet it is clear that the ministry of the word is lacking and that there is little supply both in the big meetings and in the small meetings. This problem must be solved without further delay. Food, clothing, housing, and transportation are the great necessities of life, but the most crucial necessity is food. It does not matter that much if a person's clothing is a little shabby or if his house leaks a little when it rains. His stomach, however, cannot go hungry. If a man in a certain place is hungry day after day, sooner or later he will leave that place because he will not be willing to simply wait until he dies.

Therefore, the fact that our numbers are not multiplying is eighty percent due to the scarcity of food among us and to our inability to feed people.

Even though you may not have the experience or knowledge to lead a small group, you should be able to pick up some secrets and discover some essential points by simply trying to do it. For example, a person does not have to attend a technical school to learn how to be a carpenter. By practicing carpentry under a master carpenter from his youth, he can gain experience and eventually become a master himself. Similarly, after leading a small group for a while, you should be able to discover some secrets and essential points as you attend the small group meeting. According to my general observation, the fate of the small group depends entirely upon the ministry of the word.

HOW TO LEAD THE SMALL GROUP MEETINGS

First, all of the co-workers, full-timers, elders, and core members in the small groups should be prepared to bring a suitable word as the food to the small group meetings. However, when you are preparing a word, do not consider yourselves as teachers who are going to teach some students or as elders who are going to visit and edify the saints. If you do this, you will definitely fail. Although you must be prepared, in your attitude you should still consider yourselves as students because there are no teachers or leaders in the small groups.

Next, you should not go with the intention of giving the opening word in the meeting. Although it makes a difference whether the meeting starts early or late, it is not that important. The important thing is whether or not you supply the others in the meeting and bring the riches to them. If the saints do not open the meeting in a good way, if they are only chatting, or if they sing an inappropriate hymn, then you need to properly open the meeting. If they open the meeting properly, you should simply let them carry on by themselves.

Based upon the condition of the small groups, I have realized that our leading and perfecting in the past were too weak. In the past we depended on big meetings with large numbers of people. Now, after the change of system, we have small group meetings with small numbers of people, and no one knows how to meet in this way. I have gone to several group meetings, and they were all like this. The saints were good, but they simply did not know how to meet. The reason is that in the past we were not trained in this way. The saints know how to pray, how to sing, and how to read the Scriptures, but they do not know how to apply these practices once they are in the small groups.

If we had time, I would teach you how to open the meeting, that is, how to use the hymns or the life-study messages to start the meeting. For now I can only give you some principles. In order to open the meeting in a good way, you should be able to point out the crucial items of the truth that the saints are pursuing during the week. For example, suppose that this week we are pursuing Message Ten of the *Life-study of Galatians,* and the crucial point is that it is no longer I who live, but it is Christ who lives in me. If you know this, then you can take the opportunity to lead everyone to sing *Hymns,* #499. Once the singing starts, the meeting will open up. Therefore, before you go to the small group meeting, you should familiarize yourself with the message being pursued that week and note the crucial points in it. At the small group meeting you should learn to share the crucial points with the saints. There is no need to read the whole message. Simply grasp the crucial points and feed the saints. You can also use the Bible to open the meeting by leading everyone to read the verses related to the content being pursued for the week. If no one knows how to read properly, and the reading is disorganized and disorderly, or if they do not know how to repeat-read, emphasize-read, or pray-read, then you must be the coach and think of a way to teach and perfect them so that they may learn how to read properly.

SPEAKING FOR THE LORD BEING
THE PRIMARY MATTER IN LEARNING HOW TO SERVE

Today you may be still learning how to serve full time, but this does not excuse you from knowing how to meet in the group meetings. Perhaps some would say that when they were serving full time in the past, they learned to serve in a different way. It is true that in the past I said that if you wanted to learn to serve the Lord full time, you should first start by going to the meeting hall to clean the toilets, wipe the windows, sweep the floors, and arrange the chairs. I was the one who took the lead to do these things. However, I did not intend to lead the serving ones in that way. Rather, they deviated from my way. What I meant at that time was that these matters were the basic exercises and things that we had to learn. However, that was thirty-six years ago. Today, since every hall has at least one hundred saints, is there still the need for you who are full time to wipe the chairs and clean the toilets? If you do that, you are taking over others' functions. You should let others wipe the chairs while you do other things.

I seriously hope that the elders would not lead the full-timers to go to the meeting hall and wash the windows, wipe the chairs, and clean the toilets. If the full-timers do not even have enough time or energy to take care of the small groups, then why should they be forced to take care of these lesser matters? It is true that the halls need to be cleaned, but right now what we are lacking is not people who can clean but people who can speak for the Lord. Our situation is like that of a school with many students, classrooms, and classes, but no teachers. In other words, there are many who can clean, but there are few who can teach. If the chairs in a hall are not being cleaned, this is an indication that the elders do not know how to lead the saints. This is a problem with the elders. If the elders cannot find people to wipe the windows or set up the chairs, then they should invite the saints to a love feast. After the love feast, it would be easy to ask the saints to serve. When there is love, it is easy to fellowship about anything. This is a very effective secret. This is not playing politics but helping and leading the saints by warming their hearts.

In 1939 when I was in the church in Chefoo, I would invite some saints to a love feast at the meeting hall on the nights when there were no meetings. We met on the second floor of the meeting hall, and there was a kitchen below the room where we met. I would hire a cook, not to cook meals for me but to prepare love feasts for the saints. For every love feast I would invite up to twenty guests. Eventually, all the saints had been invited to at least one love feast. Of course, my love feasts were not without a price. After being invited to a feast, many saints would do some service.

To take care of services such as ushering and cleaning the meeting hall, we only need to prepare a few love feasts for the saints. Then they will be willing to give themselves to serve and will have the heart to serve. However, the service of ministering the word cannot be taken care of simply by having a love feast. Our situation is like that of a school without teachers. We cannot simply invite a few saints over for a meal and then ask them to teach and expect them to know how to teach. Ministering the word is a most difficult thing. Every Lord's Day morning the twenty or so meeting halls in the church in Taipei have three thousand people meeting in them, all of whom are like infants crying from hunger and waiting to be fed. If we have nothing with which to supply them and no food to feed them, then we should not blame them if they do not come back the next time.

TAKING THE LEAD BUT NOT ACTING AS THE HEAD

We have been encouraging the saints to meet in small groups. They are very happy about this, but they do not know how to meet in this way. Perhaps some who were previously in the young people's meetings learned a hymn there. This may be the only hymn they know. Thus, when they come to the small group meeting, they can sing only this one hymn. Perhaps others do not know how to start the meeting, so they chat about all sorts of subjects. Therefore, if someone does not lead the meeting in a good way, then when the brothers and sisters come to the meeting, they will not know what to do. Consequently, others may receive a bad impression of our meeting and may not want to come again in the future. Moreover, once people receive a bad impression, it is hard to change this impression.

I believe this is the reason that there is no increase in the small groups. Therefore, I would like to train you to lead the small groups. In the past when we practiced having small group meetings, we made some arrangements. We arranged for certain ones to be group responsible ones, home responsible ones, and hall responsible ones. There were at least two responsible ones in a small group so that when one was sick or had other matters to take care of, the other could substitute. However, the saints began to think that to be a responsible one was to have an official position. The situation reached a point in which it was difficult to even assign responsible ones because there would always be eight or ten people competing to be a home responsible one. If we appointed only two people, then the others would get offended and would not come to the meeting for one or two months. Some would even question the elders as to why they were letting a person be responsible who was less qualified than they. Therefore, we do not want to have titles. We do not want any of the saints to act as the head.

However, if no one acts as the head, then it is hard to meet. Of course, there are some saints who have a clean heart and do not assume to be leaders. They do not want to serve as officials. They only know to love the Lord and to love the brothers and sisters. Moreover, they know how to serve and also have certain spiritual abilities. When this kind of person comes to the meeting, he spontaneously helps the brothers and sisters and supplies the meeting. As a result, the small group meeting is successful. However, suppose such a one does everything and directs everything. He is the one who calls the hymns, selects the Scripture verses, and speaks the message. Since he is spiritually weighty and experienced in life, the result will be that most of the saints will prefer to go to his small group meetings and not to the meetings in the meeting hall. This would not be a good situation either. This is why we say that this matter of taking the lead is the most difficult point.

OUR MEETINGS HINGING ON OUR SPEAKING

I have been in the Lord's work for more than fifty years. Before we changed the system this last time, I considered many times before the Lord how we would accomplish such a change. Now the change is being accomplished before our eyes. The way that the Lord is leading us on is the best way. This is not something that we dreamed into being. Rather, it is the cumulative result of our many years of experience and observation before the Lord. Regrettably, there is one troublesome matter—the number of people who can speak for the Lord is too small, and the ministry of the word in the meetings is too weak. Being able to speak for the Lord is not a matter that can be developed instantaneously.

Even though this is the case, I still feel very hopeful because of all the full-timers here. Therefore, after considering this matter before the Lord, I decided to set aside time to give you some training. I hope that after you have gone through the training, you will be able to meet the need for the ministry of the word in the group meetings. This is my burden. For me to lead one small group would not be difficult, but for me to lead four hundred groups would be difficult. At present there are one hundred full-timers. The least I can do is to set aside some time to teach you all to lead one hundred small groups. For this reason, I hope that each of you would attend a small group meeting and attend the same one regularly for your exercise and learning. Starting from today, you should not wander from group to group, drifting everywhere. Rather, you should attend the same group regularly. As to the other three hundred groups, you must leave them and let others work on them.

LEARNING IN THE SMALL GROUPS

When you go to a small group meeting, you should not have the intention or the attitude that you are there to teach. You should have only one real burden—to be a saint attending the small group meeting and learning to lead the small group meeting. It is worthwhile to learn how to lead a group meeting. The most crucial aspect of a small group meeting is the opening of the meeting. Do not open the meeting hastily, and do not compete to be the first to open the meeting. You should let the saints open the meeting. If they do not do a good job of opening the meeting, that may waste only five or six minutes. Then you can give a good opening word to help them have a good meeting. You should not speak much unless it is necessary. If you use a life-study message to open the meeting, and the saints follow by reading the message but read in a disorganized way, then you can speak a few sentences to help them. You should not set out with the intention to teach the saints, but you should take the opportunity to educate them when you have the chance. Everyone likes to learn. Even though some of the saints have been saved for many years, they may not know how to meet. Thus, you need to teach them little by little. You may not succeed immediately, for they will not learn immediately. You may have to teach them a little at a time. If you teach them a little at a time, after three or four meetings, they will learn.

Besides this, you need to learn to contact the members of the small group individually. For example, you may visit the home of the one who will be hosting the next meeting. When you go, do not go with the intent to teach him. Rather, go spontaneously before the time of the meeting. You do not need to make an appointment; simply go before the meeting begins. If the meeting starts at seven-thirty, you could go at six-thirty. When you arrive, you do not need to say, "I have come early to visit you." If he asks you why you are early, you can say, "Praise the Lord that He gave me the feeling to come early." Then you can talk with his whole family, taking the opportunity to observe their condition, to fellowship with them, and to render them the appropriate help. You could even teach the head of the household how to open up his home and how to receive the saints when they come.

You should not forget your status and your work. You are full-timers. All of your time is for the Lord and His church. Therefore, you should not be inflexible in deciding the place and time of your meals. If the meeting starts at seven-thirty, you can eat earlier in order to make it to the meeting at six-thirty. During the meeting, if you see a saint having difficulty, then you need to find an opportunity to contact him. However, do not approach him as a preacher or a teacher. You have to show concern for him and cherish him in a spontaneous way. After the contact, you may arrange to have a meal with him for fellowship before the next meeting and to attend the group meeting together. Never tell him, "I can tell that you are having difficulty, so I want to invite you for a meal and for fellowship. I hope this will help you." Rather, you should share some of your testimony with him in a very normal way or read a portion of the Word to him for him to receive the real help. This is to do the real work.

You do not need to take care of those who are in other groups. Simply endeavor to labor in your group. In this way, in less than half a year the saints in your group will surely be on track. The direct and indirect effect or influence will be indescribable and immeasurable. The number of people in your group will quickly increase, and you will be able to form another group. I believe that through this kind of fellowship you can understand what is the proper way to work.

THE SERVICE OF THE FULL-TIMERS BEING TO MEET

In your church life no service should conflict with the meetings because the church meetings are the full-timers' work. The other saints come to the meetings simply to attend, but you who are full-timers must come to serve. Therefore, you need to study how to minister to others in the meeting what you have received of the Lord and also how to care for the saints' individual needs. I do not mean that you should go and take care of everyone. You should simply take care of one specific person. Week after week you should take care of individual people, one by one. The number of people you take care of will naturally accumulate over the years. If you perfect one person every six months, then after five or ten years you will have borne fruit a hundredfold. We must have this view for our work.

Do not seek to be great in working for the Lord. Do not dream of becoming a great evangelist who holds campaigns and leads hundreds of thousands of people to be saved. That is not necessarily the way of the Lord. The Lord's way is to save people one by one. He says in the Bible, "Truly, truly, I say to you, Unless the grain of wheat falls into the ground and dies, it abides alone; but if it dies, it bears much fruit" (John 12:24). A single grain of wheat cannot produce hundreds and millions of grains in a short time. Rather, each and every grain multiplies—one thirtyfold, one sixtyfold, and one a hundredfold (Matt. 13:8, 23). The result is that a little multiplication accumulates to produce a great abundance. Today I am very happy because there are over a hundred full-timers here. It would be a tremendous thing if each of you went and earnestly led and worked on a group.

We have been promoting the small groups for eight months already but with no result. Generally speaking, this is because no one knows what to do, and due to our complacency, everyone simply lets the time go by week after week. Therefore, to this day our situation has been unremarkable and ordinary. Nothing new has happened. If all of us had known how to work for the Lord and had endeavored to work well, then during the past eight months, our numbers would have at least doubled from one hundred groups to two hundred. However, the situation has not been so.

LEARNING TO ADJUST AS THE SITUATION DEMANDS

It is actually not that hard to carry out the small groups. We simply need to learn to adjust as the situation demands. Those who have been trained by me can testify that what I teach in the training and what we do in actual practice are sometimes different. This is because in the actual carrying out of what is taught, we sometimes have to adjust due to practical needs. A good coach teaches his students according to regulation, but at the same time he also teaches them that when they are carrying out what is taught, they need to be able to adjust according to the demands of the situation. For example, a boxer may box with his coach during practice in a particular way. However, if he uses exactly the same movements at a competition, he will lose. If his coach were to box in a competition, he would not box in exactly the same manner as he boxes while practicing. Instead, he will adjust as the situation demands and will win. This is the coach's wisdom.

Let us use driving as another example. We must follow the traffic rules and regulations when learning to drive. However, when we are on the road, we need to be able to adjust to the conditions on the road. Otherwise, an accident might happen.

This is the challenge. When you are teaching someone to drive, you should give him some teaching materials. If you do not give him any materials containing various principles, then you will not be able to teach him. It is good to teach the regulations during the class and during training, but when it comes to the actual driving, the driver must learn to adjust according to the situation and apply what he has learned to the appropriate environment. The same is true with translation. A word can be interpreted many ways, and one needs to make the best judgment based upon the context and logic of the facts. For you to begin working on a group, I can only teach you the principles. You have to endeavor to get into the details and to put them into practice. Then the results will be unlimited. In doing anything, you cannot be so rigid. It is the same with leading a small group. You need to adjust according to the situation, and you need to properly apply what you have learned.

This situation is a perfect opportunity for you. I have given you the way and the principles. You need to hold on to these, be diligent to carry them out, and learn to adjust according to the situation. I believe that if you do this, you will see some results, even if your results are not complete.

SERVING IN THE NEW WAY ORDAINED BY GOD

As ones who have come out to serve full time, you should serve in the new way ordained by God. Do not think that to serve full time is to learn to stand on a platform and give messages. This concept is wrong. In the past we could not maintain the Lord's Day meeting without someone giving a message. However, now we are not depending on you to give messages on the platform. Rather, we want you to contact people. If you are willing to spend five years to attend as many church meetings as possible and to learn to serve, using half of every day to learn the truth and the other half to work, then the future of the Lord's recovery will definitely be bright.

There are many ways by which we can work. We can work by contacting the members in a small group or the saints attending the meeting. It is not necessary for others to give you a charge and a commission. Rather, you should already have this view that your work is to happily and voluntarily contact others and then to fellowship with them in a normal way by either inviting them for a meal or visiting them in their homes to cherish and help them. If you would do this for months and even years, the result would be inestimable.

You must realize that your work is not like a carpenter's work, which cannot reproduce itself. What you are working on is something that reproduces itself. Today you may be laboring on eight people, all of whom can reproduce. In the beginning the Lord created only one couple, but the issue of this one couple has been a continual multiplication and increase. Now after six thousand years there are billions of people. If in the beginning the Lord had created a chair, today there would still be only one chair. So do not view your caring for eight people as a light matter. It may be that one of them will become a leading apostle and be greatly used by the Lord. Who can say that this will not happen? I hope that you would all be in this new, God-ordained way, endeavoring to learn how to serve.

It is a big mistake to overemphasize a particular service and to neglect the church meetings. This is acceptable occasionally but not for a prolonged period of time. Since the meetings are your work and service, in scheduling your time you should make sure that your particular service does not occupy the meeting times. You have to meet because the meetings are your work. Of course, one of those meetings should be the small group meeting. I hope that every one of you would diligently labor and care for one small group.

SERVING AND LEADING IN A SPECIFIC SERVICE

Since I have not observed your specific services, I am not quite familiar with your situations. Thus, I can only give you some principles. I believe that these principles are right and are according to the ideal concept as well as the proper spiritual theories. First, regardless of whether we are serving with the junior high, high school, or college students, the first goal should be to get people saved. We should get people saved in an aggressive way. Following a person's salvation, we should not bring him to the meeting hall to mop the floor or wipe the windows. Instead, we should lead him to preach the gospel and encourage him to lead others to salvation. This should be their service, even their primary service. After getting a student saved, we should not bring him to the meeting hall to join a service group. That would be wrong. Even if a person has the time and the heart to join a service group, this kind of leading would be wrong. These newly saved ones, because they are students, should be encouraged only to endeavor to preach the gospel to get others saved. This should be their service.

How to Bring the Junior High and High School Students into the Church Life

We need to have a proper view of the church life. When we arranged the specific services, we pointed out that the students should attend the meetings at the hall that is closest to their school. Therefore, when a student gets saved, we have to do our best to encourage him to do this. We should introduce him to the hall that is closest to his school. In this way he will become one of the saints belonging to that hall. This will also make it convenient for the students to come together for fellowship after school. Of course this matter will not be very easy to work out because the junior high students and the high school students have very tight study schedules. Most of them also live at home and must go home after school. It is also hard for them to go out during the weekends. Regarding this point, we must be flexible and know how to adjust according to the need of the situation.

For example, first we must bring them to the Lord's table meeting. It would be best if they could attend the Lord's table meeting on the Lord's Day. If they cannot do so (for example, if their parents would not allow them to come), then we can arrange to meet at an appropriate time during the week after school and lead them to break bread at a saint's home near the school. We have to learn to lead them to remember the Lord properly. Whether we do this or not will make a big difference. We need to lead them to come together to break bread and teach them to understand what the breaking of bread is and what its significance is. This is part of their church life.

When we do this, we need to learn to adapt to others, helping them according to their situation. If I was a parent, I probably would not allow my children to go out on the Lord's Day because they already go to school six days out of the week, so it is not so suitable for them to go out on their day off. Therefore, in order to adapt to their situations, we could have a meeting to remember the Lord on a weekday in the early evening at a saint's home near the school and lead ten or twenty of them to break the bread. By doing this, we will bring them into the church life and make that meeting a part of the church. This will give them a deep impression.

The Principles of Serving with College Students

Not Using the Worldly Ways

Concerning the service with the college students, we should not use the worldly ways too much. Instead, we should try our best to avoid them. I understand that a certain way may appear to be quite good, but in reality it may not necessarily be good. Let us use the recent gospel meetings as an example. On the invitation and tracts someone used the expression *gospel speeches*. This is improper in two ways. First, the term *speeches* is too worldly, and second, it is somewhat dishonest to use this term, because in reality we are not giving speeches but preaching the gospel. To say that our gospel meetings are for giving speeches is too much. If we are so accommodating, then as we go on, what seemed like a slight error in the beginning will result in a big mistake in the end. This is what I am concerned about.

Emphasizing the Truth

Second, I hope that we would focus on the truth in carrying out the gospel work. For instance, consider one of the hymns that someone composed. It says, "Having Jesus, I have a song, I have love, I have the way." These kinds of words, along with the melody used for this hymn, will surely touch the young people, but the truth is lacking. Always keep in mind that the power of the gospel depends on prayer and the word. For the preaching of the gospel to be powerful, we must pray. In this way when we speak about sin, we will be able to shake people's hearts and move people to tears. I would love to see many young people shedding tears and repenting after hearing the preaching of the gospel and some speaking about sin for ten minutes. This is the best and most proper way. Paying attention only to outward ways in order to stir up people may not be wrong, but it also may not be very good. These ways cause people to be excited, but there is no truth in them as a foundation. If we depend only on these ways, our work will be like a castle built in the air—something empty, vain, and without a foundation.

We have to be trained in our speaking. If we are speaking about the existence of God, then we need to "hammer" the knowledge of God and the consciousness of God's existence into people. If we are speaking concerning sin, then we need to prove to people that the nature of sin and the consciousness of sin are within them so that they will be convicted. One time George Whitefield spoke about the lake of fire. His speaking was so intense that a man in the audience grabbed on to the nearest post and said that he feared terribly that he was falling into the lake of fire right at that very moment. Such a person would surely be saved. If we only pay attention to stirring up a person's emotions, singing that Jesus is our song, our love, and our way, then this person may get excited and even be baptized, but soon his excitement will vanish, and nothing will remain in him.

The work of the Spirit follows the Lord's word. Without the Lord's word, there cannot be the work of the Spirit. The Lord has given us the Bible, which is His word. Fifty years ago we had a co-worker who, before he was saved, always despised Christianity. One day, due to a certain matter, he went up to a mountain and entered into a temple. He saw a large Bible lying open on the table of sacrifice. Out of curiosity he walked over to the Bible to see what it said. He saw that the Bible was turned to Psalm 1, and after reading it two or three times, he was captured by the Lord's word and was moved. No one preached the gospel to him or said anything to him. He was convicted by the Spirit simply by reading the word of the Lord. Ultimately, he rolled on the floor, wept, repented, and was saved. This kind of salvation is genuine. Those who are saved in this way are more trustworthy than those who are brought in through gimmicks.

If we take a shortcut or a cheap way, eventually our work will come to nothing. If we have the assurance that we can still labor on and plant seeds in those whom we have brought in, then perhaps it is all right to use a certain way. Using music that makes people very excited outwardly will not work. Do not say that all young people enjoy music. This should not be our excuse. To use a hymn at the beginning of a meeting and then to sow the seeds of the truth along with it is acceptable. We must by all means sow the truth into people. Otherwise, their salvation will not be solid.

For the preaching of the gospel, we must spend time and energy to get into the truth, to have thorough prayer, and to labor in the Lord's word. We cannot depend only on the outward things. This does not mean that we cannot use outward things as means or instruments. For example, the hall used for the meetings is something outward, and the microphone that amplifies a person's voice is also outward. However, using these outward things requires careful consideration. For example, I may use the microphone to preach the truth to you, or I may also use it to sing to you. In both cases I am using the microphone, yet what a difference there is! Consider the gospel camps or outdoor camps as another example. We may use these camps as a way to contact people. However, when we employ these things, we must stay within a limit and not be excessive or go overboard. To illustrate, it is normal to eat rice using a bowl. However, suppose you invite someone over for a meal, and since you are particular about the kind of bowl you use, you put out a bowl with beautiful patterns but with no rice within. How then will the guest be satisfied? You must put rice into the bowl. This is the limit.

WORKING FOR THE LORD REQUIRING WISDOM

Whatever the Lord has established has great significance and value. Many people consider the breaking of bread to be a light matter. In reality, however, this is a very serious matter. Throughout the ages the Catholic Church and the Protestant denominations have all paid great attention to this matter. The Catholic Church depends heavily on the mass to retain people. If the mass were taken away from the Catholic Church, they would lose half of their congregation. The mass is the meeting for the breaking of bread in the Catholic Church. Even though many matters in the Catholic Church have been confused, this matter of bread-breaking is still highly regarded. We also need to regard this matter instead of disregarding it. We need to bring a person to the bread-breaking meeting, preferably at the meeting hall on the first Lord's Day following his baptism. If in the long run he cannot go to the meeting hall that often, then we should find a place for him to break bread according to his need.

Generally speaking, we should find a suitable home near the school of the newly saved students so that we may bring them to the Lord's table meeting. This is the proper church life. The students' primary service is to preach the gospel. It would be marvelous if there could be a home near each campus so that we could have the breaking of bread with ten or fifteen people. Of course, it would be the best if we could bring them to the meeting hall, but if the circumstances do not allow this, then we should know how to be flexible and accommodating and not so rigid.

My dissatisfaction with the co-workers is that they are too rigid in their work and do not know how to be flexible. All of the worldly people who do business must learn to be flexible. The Lord Jesus said, "For the sons of this age are more prudent in their dealings with their own generation than the sons of light" (Luke 16:8). Once I heard a true story about a brother among us who owned a women's hat shop in Hong Kong. One day a celebrity came to the shop to buy a hat, and this brother waited on her. She looked at a number of hats but was not satisfied. This brother immediately said that there were better ones in the back. He then took one of the hats that she had examined and went to the back of the shop. He took off the ribbon, pressed the hat into a different mold, put on a new ribbon, and brought it back out. He said to her, "This hat is the best one." After she saw it, she bought it, paying a few times more for it than the original price.

I hope that the co-workers would learn from this story. The sons of this age are more prudent than the sons of light in worldly matters. The reason the co-workers are not doing well in their work is that they do not know how to make adjustments according to the demands of the situation. Some co-workers blame me, asking why I changed after going to the United States. Actually, I have not changed; my ways have changed. This is just like the fact that the hat in the story did not change, but the mold into which it was pressed and the ribbon that was tied around it were different. I am not being proud, but I ask you, "What is the present condition of the work of the co-workers who rebuked and opposed me in the past?" They have not produced one church. There were two who opposed me the most—one took the lead to accuse me of teaching heresy, and the other opposed me in a refined way. The two of them, one wild and the other refined, have been opposing me for thirty years, yet neither has produced a single church. However, while they have been opposing me, I have been preaching the word for the last thirty years and have produced five hundred churches.

I have no intention to boast. There are over one hundred churches in Mindanao, the southern part of the Philippines, that were raised up through the sixty topics of the *Fundamental Truths in the Scriptures*. There was one Chinese-speaking brother who moved there from Fukien when he was very young. After he was saved, he read the *Fundamental Truths in the Scriptures* and felt that it was very good. He then translated it into Visayan, which is the local dialect of the Philippines. One day he told me that it was through this set of books that he raised up one hundred churches in Mindanao. When I visited the Philippines, he told me that the saints in Mindanao are now reading the life-study messages. In South America, Brazil also has fifty to sixty churches now, and in Central America there are one hundred churches. All of these churches were raised up in the last twenty years.

Dear saints, we must be those who "bring life to a dying

business" and not be those who "bring death to a thriving business." Sometimes I feel that the co-workers are like the latter kind of people. I do not mean to criticize. I truly hope that the younger generation would change the tradition and be wise and educated in the matter of working for the Lord. What is the church life? The church life is not something stiff and dead. For a meeting to be considered a part of the church life we do not have to bring the saints to the meeting hall. I am not saying that we should not bring people to the meeting hall. What I mean is that the church life does not necessarily have to be experienced in the meeting hall. If there is a saint's house near the campus with a living room that can take up to fifteen people, and that saint is willing to open up his home for the students, then we can bring the students to have the Lord's table there, and we can care for the students there.

NEEDING TO HAVE A BROAD VISION

Regarding the one hundred of you who are full-timers, besides leading the students to break bread and preach the gospel, you also need to lead a small group meeting. You need to visit each home of the members in the group so that the group can bring in people. Thus, not only will your busyness be meaningful, but it will also produce obvious results. This should be your church life. In this way the students who break bread in the homes will be specifically cared for as well as properly perfected. Spontaneously, they will be brought into the church life and become part of the church. This is the kind of view and the way of serving you should have.

Of course, whatever you intend to do, you need to fellowship with the elders first. You have to explain everything to them and receive their confirmation. I would say to the elders that your view has to be broadened. Do not focus only on the numbers, and do not say that everyone who is saved must come and meet in the meeting hall. Actually, they can go anywhere because they have been saved by the Lord and are in the Lord's church. I hope that the number of students living the church life under the care of the full-timers would eventually be greater than the number of saints living the church life in the meeting hall. The elders should not care whether or not the full-timers bring the students to the Lord's table at the meeting hall. The crucial thing is that they must do their work in a proper manner and gain results. I am not saying that the older saints and the working saints are not precious. Nevertheless, for the future of the Lord's recovery, our burden is still for the students. Since nearly all of the full-timers will come from the college campuses, we should bring in the students. The more students we bring in, the better.

What I have fellowshipped is in the nature of principles. We need to endeavor to study these matters further. In conclusion, there are three points—first, we must use the truth to bring people to salvation; second, we must lead them to break bread; and third, we must lead them to serve by preaching the gospel to save people. The table meeting should not be too long. It should be one hour at most, with fifteen minutes for singing and bread-breaking and then forty-five minutes for a message and sharing. May the Lord grant us mercy that we may have the wisdom to do His work.

EXERCISING COMPREHENSIVE CARE
IN THE ARRANGEMENT OF THE SERVICES

Regarding the matter of taking care of the small groups, I hope that you would exercise comprehensive care for the entire leading of the new way. If for your specific service you are leading the students to break bread, caring for a small group, and having personal contact with others, then you should do only the campus work. This is a part of the church life. However, if you still have energy, then you should also serve the saints who meet at the meeting hall in addition to your specific service, faithfully serving in the small group at the meeting hall and helping the small group to go on. If there is the need, you may also lead the small group to break bread. This is also part of the church life. It all depends on how you do it.

THE STANDARD FOR
THE BROTHERS' AND SISTERS' HOUSES

The brothers' and sisters' houses may also be used for edification and perfection. Many of the high school and college students are from out of town and need a place to live. The brothers' and sisters' houses would not only solve the matter of where to live, they would also serve the purpose of providing a place for mutual edification. You could also use the brothers' and sisters' houses as places for the breaking of bread. Everything depends on how you do it.

GRASPING THE OPPORTUNITY
TO PURSUE AGGRESSIVELY AND TO BE EQUIPPED

All those who have become full time have done so in order to learn. If I were to leave you here and not care about you, I would be doing you an injustice. I hope that you would all endeavor individually, especially in studying the truth, learning how to read the Word and how to pray, and pursuing the growth in life. This is something that no one can do for you. You all have studied in school, and you know that regardless of how much your parents love you, they cannot study for you. You yourself must study. Therefore, in reading the Word, praying, and pursuing the growth in life, you have to endeavor on your own.

I truly feel that the Lord has given us an open door in Taiwan. I grew up in Christianity and saw how difficult it was for the Western missionaries who did not have a door opened to them. All over China people simply did not want the gospel. The Western missionaries were called the "big devils," and the Chinese who received Christianity were called the "second devils." During the Boxer Rebellion in 1900, rioters killed the "big devils" and the "second devils." My mother tore down all the gospel banners in our house and escaped to the mountains. Those were truly difficult times. Therefore, when one door was opened to a Western missionary, it was considered very precious. Not only so, the majority of those who received the Lord were mostly laborers, unskilled laborers, and the poor. Almost none of them were educated. However, today in Taipei we do not have to spend much effort to get over a hundred people to come and hear the gospel. If we worked harder, we could get dozens of people baptized. Right now the door is open, but the workers are inadequate.

It is not the number of workers that is insufficient but the ministry of the word that is inadequate.

I do not like to do anything that excites people. However, now I want to stir up the elders to become full time. What the churches need the most at this time are full-time elders. The church in Taipei has around eighty elders. I hope that at least forty of them would become full time. In this way there would be two full-time elders in every hall. Then if the church in Taipei still does not accomplish anything, there will be no excuse. In order to accomplish something, there needs to be full-timers. The standard of living in Taiwan is going up. If the elders who hold jobs do not work hard and make progress at their jobs, then they will be fired. So you have to sympathize with the elders because they truly do not have much time to serve. If the elders want to have time to serve, then they should become full time. The church definitely needs elders to give themselves to serve full time. Their living should be supported by the church. In this way the church can have a future. Otherwise, nothing will be accomplished. Therefore, we need to pray much for this matter.

We hope that on the whole island of Taiwan five hundred young people would begin to serve full time every year. Thus, in five years there would be 2,500 full-timers to meet the goal of the five-year gospelization of Taiwan. This is a difficult task. We need to pray for this, and everyone in the church must take action and give themselves for this. Not only must the saints give their whole being, but the financial support also has to come in. Only in this way can we go on. Otherwise, no matter how hard we push, nothing will move.

I believe that these matters will not be problems to us. As long as we are faithful to move forward, the Lord will be responsible. I am very experienced in this matter. For the past sixty years I have experienced that our Lord is trustworthy and faithful. He will never fail us. The most difficult thing is to produce those who can speak for the Lord. Therefore, I hope that we would grasp this opportunity and exercise to speak for the Lord, not by giving messages on a platform but by leading the small groups and by contacting the saints individually. As far as the service for the campus work is concerned, we should try our best to lead the students to have the Lord's table and then lead them to also preach the gospel. In this way the Lord will have a way to go on.

CHAPTER THREE

THE LEARNING IN THE FULL-TIME TRAINING

THE TRANSLATION WORK OF
THE NEW TESTAMENT RECOVERY VERSION

During the past two to three years, the matter that I have been most concerned with and that has required a great deal of consideration has been the translation work regarding the Chinese New Testament Recovery Version. In Taiwan, the United States, and Southeast Asia, there has been an urgent and pressing call for a better translation of the New Testament. However, this matter, because it is related to the wording of the Bible, cannot be done in an ordinary way. This is not an easy matter that we are undertaking. Even someone who is knowledgeable and well-versed in Chinese, English, and Greek may not necessarily do a good job. When I was in Southeast Asia recently, I met a group of saints who were familiar with both Chinese and English and were serving specifically in the translation of the literature for the churches. They translated the outlines of my Chinese messages into English. I did not think that there would be any problem with this. However, before I was about to release the messages in English, I read the English outlines and realized that there were major differences between the two versions. The problem was not that the translators had a poor command of English or Chinese but that they did not understand the terms used in the Lord's recovery. Therefore, I was reminded all the more that I cannot be careless in this matter.

To translate the Bible requires a substantial knowledge of the truth and also a great deal of careful consideration. Bible translators throughout the ages have not been able to accurately grasp the original meaning of the Bible or fully understand the principles of the Bible, even though many of them were highly educated people. We cannot understand the Bible or even the text of a verse according to its words alone. Although the words are important—without words, everything is vague—what is more important is that we understand the spiritual matters and be familiar with the principles of the Bible itself. If we are short of the knowledge concerning spiritual matters, have an inadequate understanding of the biblical principles and their interrelationships, are unable to grasp the basic truths of the Bible, and understand the Bible merely according to the letter, then it will be easy for us to make mistakes.

Concerning the letter of the Bible, the Old Testament was written in Hebrew and the New Testament was written in Greek. Even though these two written languages have been developing for thousands of years, the meanings of the words themselves are still very hard to understand. In Greek one word alone sometimes has more than ten different meanings and many different usages. The biblical truths in the Old Testament are not hard to understand, but those in the New Testament are altogether in the heavenly realm. Therefore, to decide on the meaning of a word in a verse is not an easy matter.

After I was saved, I began to love studying the Bible, especially the New Testament. During the past twelve years I had to write the footnotes for the New Testament Recovery Version in order to release the life-study messages. This forced me to touch each crucial word in the Bible in a thorough way.

Nearly all the crucial points in the Bible are now within me. Therefore, having further examined the publications put out by our bookroom, I am deeply concerned that if those who are involved in the translation of the Bible do not have an accurate understanding of the original meanings of the words in the Bible, then their translation will surely contain mistakes. Hence, after careful consideration I have decided to labor on this personally by taking the lead in the translation of the New Testament Recovery Version, and I hope that we can complete this project as soon as possible.

Since you are being trained to be useful for the work of the

Lord's recovery, you need to be familiar with at least two languages—your mother tongue, Chinese, and the universal language, English. Learning these languages will require you to spend time and energy. In order to learn the English language, you can practice studying not only the New Testament Recovery Version but also the King James Version, which does not contain too many new words or sophisticated phrases. Most people appreciate the depth of its English. Those who are pursuing to learn the English language cannot bypass the King James Version. Many have tried to replace it with other English versions because its history is over three hundred years old and because it contains some phrases or terms that are somewhat out of date. However, no version has been able to replace it. When we were working on the English New Testament Recovery Version, we did not depart too much from the King James Version. We did our best to preserve its style and use its phrases, clauses, and words, unless they did not match the meaning of the original text. Therefore, the language of the English New Testament Recovery Version is not too sophisticated and should be easy for you to get into. This will be a great help to you.

KNOWING THE LORD'S RECOVERY

In this message I am going to give you a comprehensive word as a guide for your exercise during your time in the training.

The Lord's recovery is surely of the Lord. This means that we believe in the Lord, follow Him, serve Him, and bear the testimony of the church for Him altogether according to the pure revelation of the holy Scriptures. In the past we examined the characteristics of various Christian denominations, such as how much they accepted the Bible, how they practiced the Christian living, and how they set up churches. We did not accept their practices right away, regardless of what kinds of practices they had. Instead, we brought their practices before the Bible and compared them with the revelation in the Bible. We accepted only that which was according to the Bible, trying to accept as much as possible. Although we were born not in the first or second century but in the twentieth century, through our thorough research and our open-mindedness we have received nearly everything that measures up to the Bible. Therefore, we have received much help. We can say that the way of the Lord's recovery today is altogether according to the Bible and not according to the two thousand years of Christian tradition.

The University of the Philippines, as the highest national institute of education in the Philippines, gathers the country's top students. There was a professor of agricultural technology who was saved among us and who saw the way of the church while pursuing his doctoral degree in the United States. After returning to the Philippines, he started teaching at this university. He bore a strong testimony for the Lord and led almost everyone around him to salvation. Within only four years, the testimony of the church was raised up in that locality. There were about forty saints meeting together, and almost all of them were in the field of education. Some of the saints were his colleagues and teaching assistants, and others were his students and friends. There were also some middle school teachers.

When I visited the Philippines recently, I visited this church. The saints told me that the agriculture department at the University of the Philippines has seven thousand students and that there are fourteen Christian organizations, mostly from the United States, that are carrying out campus works among the students to gain the campus. The saints specifically pointed out that most of these fourteen organizations oppose us. Furthermore, in opposing us they take the same way used in the United States—whomever we contact receives the slanderous book *The God-Men* the following day. The brothers had been doing their best to defend the truth. I asked them if they had used the "Statement of Decision" issued by the court in relation to the lawsuit we had filed in the United States, and they said that they had not. They had only used some articles printed in the newspaper. I told them that this was not enough and that they had to utilize the "Statement of Decision." After they published a defending statement of rebuttal in the newspaper, one pastor wrote a letter to us, saying that our rebuttal was excellent and that the only defect was that our truths were not according to tradition. I told the brothers that this was the best kind of praise. The truths that we teach are definitely not according to tradition but according to the pure words of the Bible. So I had the brothers tell that pastor that if he wanted to debate with us, he would have to use the Bible, because that is what we respect. We would disregard any debate with us that is based upon the Nicene Creed or the things of tradition.

Many of the beliefs in today's Protestantism, and even more in Catholicism, are not according to the Bible but according to the so-called councils. Some in Christianity believe that the decisions of the councils surpass the teachings of the Bible. Therefore, instead of saying, "This is what the Bible says," they say, "This is what the councils decided." The first council was the Nicene Council of A.D. 325, presided over by Constantine the Great. Afterward, in A.D. 570, the papal system was officially recognized, and the pope replaced the councils. Before the recognition of the papal system, all the controversies over spiritual matters were settled according to the decisions of the councils. Throughout the generations much of Christianity has been saying, "Thus says the councils," and not, "Thus says the Bible."

The Lord's recovery, however, is different. We declared from the beginning that we were absolutely not according to tradition and that we did not care for the Christian councils prior to the establishment of the papal system. We have come back to the pure word of God. Regardless of how good the teachings of the Christian councils and the traditional theology are, as long as they do not correspond to the Bible, we reject them. We are only for the pure word of God.

Since you are attending the Full-Time Training, as a rule, you should be trained in the matter of knowing the church. This means that you should learn to come back to the pure and accurate word of God to see what the church is and what the way, the ground, the practice, and the content of the church are. I hope that you all would know these points clearly. We have many books regarding these matters, but regrettably, they have not been compiled in a systematic way. Rather, the books contain one point here and another point there. Presently, we are compiling the *Truth Lessons* and are preparing to publish them in four levels. Each level will consist of forty-eight topics. The purpose is to systematically arrange all the literature that we have published in the past sixty years so that the saints can have a summarized and clear understanding of the truth.

PURSUING PROGRESS IN OUR SERVICE

Proverbs 29:18 begins, "Where there is no vision, the people cast off restraint." If we do not have a clear vision, it will be hard for us to pursue progress in our service. Without the stimulus of competition, worldly people would be without a goal and would be eliminated. It would be hard for someone opening a factory to achieve anything if he did not think of a way to gain the market. Even though we are not opening a factory for business, the principle is the same for us who are doing the Lord's work. We have the highest truth and the practice that most agrees with the Bible. However, if we are ignorant, boastful, closed to the outside world, and do not pursue progress, then the Lord will not have a way among us.

In order to propagate and increase, some people in the Catholic Church have accepted the so-called Pentecostal movement. Once I researched and attended this kind of Pentecostal meeting. I went to a meeting where they used the word *charismatic* instead of *Pentecostal* at their door. In the meeting the Catholic priests wore their priestly robes and the nuns wore the nuns' garments. However, they did not sit in an orderly way. Some prostrated themselves and others sat on the floor. There was no one presiding over the meeting, nor was there a preacher. The believers simply stood up one by one to testify and share, and then at the end someone made some announcements regarding practical affairs.

Their way is very smart. It is known as the moderate charismatic movement. They approve of speaking in tongues, and they practice speaking in tongues, but in the meetings they do not do it, nor do they force others to do it. Furthermore, they do not perform miracles and wonders. They simply encourage the believers to share and testify how they have touched and enjoyed the Lord. This kind of practice touches people's hearts. Moreover, they do not put any demands on the believers; they do not even demand that they attend the Lord's Day meeting and testify. Therefore, it is easy for them to bring people in.

Our difficulty is that we are not only hoping to bring people in but are also hoping to bring them into the church life. Surely we need to bring people into the church life, but this requires us to endeavor step by step. We have to work harder because we not only ask the saints to meet but also expect them to meet according to a schedule. The dear elders in the churches even expect the saints to participate in practical services such as cleaning the meeting hall, cleaning the restrooms, and giving hospitality. Many people are willing to believe in Jesus, but they are not willing to clean the meeting hall and the restrooms. The charismatic Catholics normally rent their meeting halls. They hire people to clean the place so that it is very neat and clean. Even the restrooms look very nice. Therefore, their members are responsible only for coming to the meetings and do not have to worry about anything else. However, although they spend time together in the Lord's Day meeting, the remainder of their time is spent going to movies, window-shopping, and playing games. We cannot condemn them, though, because quality comes out of quantity. The charismatic Christians have been able to bring in so many people. Thus, we cannot deny the fact that there has been a certain amount of the work of the Holy Spirit among them.

Today one cannot do business or operate a factory in an isolated way. Rather, one must learn from and investigate others' practices and absorb others' strong points in order to succeed. The Japanese do a very thorough job in this matter. Regardless of what line of business they are in, the first thing they do is send people to foreign countries to learn from others. They then come back and have a meeting to compare and absorb all the good points and strong points from each country. This is why their products can be marketed to countries all over the world, occupying the international market. The co-workers among us who are fifty years old or above are not like this; they are closed to everything except the truth.

They do not care about anything and do not want to learn anything besides the truth. Consequently, there has been no progress. Today we are unaware that there are many groups that are far more advanced than we are, and we are also unaware of where we are. My burden is very heavy. Basically, I hope that all you trainees would clearly understand the way we are taking and also aggressively pursue progress in the matter of service.

PURSUING THE KNOWLEDGE OF THE TRUTH

First, the serving ones in the recovery must pursue progress in their service; second, they must pursue the knowledge of the truth. This is an area in which we have had the upper hand for the past sixty years. This is true even in the United States today. Unfortunately, the co-workers whom I trained thirty years ago have not sufficiently entered into the deeper study of the truth. They are able to give messages, but they cannot get into the depths of the truth. Not only so, some co-workers even feel that since we speak only on messages given by Brother Nee and Brother Lee, it would not be a bad idea to find some materials from others to speak on. This kind of understanding and feeling is altogether wrong.

The Lord's speaking today is mostly in His recovery, yet we do not cherish it. People outside the recovery use the truths that have been released among us in a serious way, yet we who are in the recovery are indifferent toward these truths. There is a certain group which holds educational classes on the Lord's Day. The believers who join the class must register and take a test, and no one can join the class in the middle of the course. Everyone in the special class has the book *The Normal Christian Life,* and they study it seriously. The author of that book is Brother Watchman Nee, and I wrote the preface. If you asked the people in this class whether they know Watchman Nee or Witness Lee, they probably would not recognize those names. However, each person has a copy of the book and is learning the truth from it. Few of us, however, possess the entire set of life-study messages. Others love the truths in the Lord's recovery to such an extent, but what is our attitude toward the truths that the Lord has given us?

By glancing through the outline of the Bible study put out by that group, one can immediately recognize that they are using our material. For example, the outline for Romans 1 talks about the three "giving-ups" (vv. 24, 26, 28). This was not my personal invention. Rather, I started seeing this while I was with the Brethren. I was taught by the Brethren when I was young. Then I brought what they had taught me into the Lord's recovery. I published my writings in the *Life-study of Romans* over ten years ago. Some young co-workers wrote to me a few years ago, telling me that they had visited the churches in Europe and America and had been influenced to study others' writings. After their return, they took many different expositions and compared them with our life-study messages. Eventually, they concluded that all the materials out there cannot be compared to ours. In spite of this, we still do not appreciate the Lord's speaking among us as much as others do.

You need to clearly know this way—the way of the recovery. If you do not know the way of the recovery clearly, I would advise you not to remain in it. Rather, you might as well take the free way of Christianity. However, even if you know the way clearly, you still need to know the truth and enter into the light that the Lord has given to us over the past sixty years. The light from these sixty years is a collection of what all the pursuers of the Lord in the past two thousand years of church history have understood concerning the Bible. Although we do not have as many publications as Christianity does, our publications are at the top. I am very confident about this matter. I have already told you that our writings were produced by our standing on the shoulders of many who studied the Bible during the past two thousand years, plus what the Lord has shown us. You need to make an effort to study them in a deeper way.

Perhaps you may have some understanding of the basic truths of the Bible, but you probably have not spent much effort to study them. To study any course of learning is not that easy. You need to know the achievements of the masters throughout the ages. You need to spend time entering into their writings in order to reap the benefit. I hope you will treat the truth among us in this way, spending time to enter into it.

PURSUING PROGRESS IN LIFE

The third thing that the serving ones in the recovery must do is to pursue progress in life. This means that you must first endeavor to know the Spirit, Christ, life, the cross, and resurrection. Then you should have the practical experience of all these things. As long as you have the heart to do so, it will not be difficult to practice this matter. There are many books among us concerning the knowledge and experience of life. If these writings had been available sixty years ago, I would have been excited to spend all my time storing up all these riches within me. Unfortunately, at that time I could not find one book that even explained the truth of regeneration. We, however, have studied this matter of regeneration in a thorough way. Of course, we received help from a word given by Brother T. Austin-Sparks. He said that regeneration is to receive a life in addition to the life that we already have. Based on this word, we have further developed this matter. Among all of the books in Christianity today, the ones that give the clearest explanation of regeneration are our books.

To pursue the progress in life, you must study *The Knowledge of Life*. The more times you read it the better. Then you need to study the book *The Experience of Life*. It would be good to read this book once every two years and to actually practice what it teaches regarding both the dealings in life and the learning in life. These two books contain the messages that I gave during the trainings in 1953 and 1954. They were first published in a series in *The Ministry of the Word*. The brother who wrote the preface said that throughout the generations many people had spoken about life and had taught about life but did not know what life was, not to mention the experience of life. It was I who used the scientific method to completely present what so many throughout the generations had taught and experienced, plus my own experience. So I hope that you would all study it diligently.

I will not train you as I did in the former days. We already have the richest and most complete truths among us. Thus, there is no need for me to speak more to you. Instead, I will use the method of graduate study to teach you, that is, to let you study the reference books and then to test you. It would be more than sufficient if you collected all the books published among us from the time of Brother Nee until today and seriously studied them one by one.

One matter that truly worries me is that those of you who are being trained here all want to do something special. This truly grieves my heart. I worked with Brother Nee in China for eighteen years. I was completely one with him. I spoke what he spoke, and I preached what he preached. I even imitated his gestures. There was no difference between us. Anyone can testify for me that wherever I went, I did not speak on other topics but only repeated to the brothers and sisters the messages that Brother Nee had released. I am proud of this. However, I found out that this is not the situation among my co-workers. Rather, everyone wants to have his own "new tricks" and "new gimmicks," not realizing that it is these new things that delay the Lord's work.

I never tried to play tricks or use gimmicks. Rather, I simply worked with all my effort to compare and study the Bible in its original language, in Chinese, and in English, and then to find the basic truths and present them. I hope that you also would not try to invent new things. Simply absorb these basic truths and teach them accordingly. Concerning the pursuit of life, what other books are more basic than *The Knowledge of Life* and *The Experience of Life*? What other book can speak as clearly and transparently as the chapter on the three laws and four lives in *The Knowledge of Life*? These books are like the multiplication table; they are very basic and cannot be replaced with a new gimmick. If you teach multiplication, you must use the multiplication table. Do not think that you do not have to teach it because it has already been taught by others. This kind of thinking truly causes my heart to ache.

I do not have the time to speak all these things to you again. You have to understand that all the basic items are in the books. All you have to do is to study them thoroughly. In particular, you must spend time and energy to get into *The*

Knowledge of Life and *The Experience of Life.* I have decided to incorporate all the points covered in these two books into the forty-eight lessons of the *Truth Lessons.* I hope that you will all be able to have a solid pursuit and progress in life.

LEARNING HOW TO CONDUCT YOURSELF, HOW TO DO THINGS, AND HOW TO WORK

The fourth point is that you need to learn how to conduct yourself, how to do things, and how to work. This point is all-inclusive. When I was here holding the training thirty years ago, I once said, "If you do not know how to conduct yourself, you will not know how to do things, and if you do not know how to do things, you will not know how to work." I called this the "three how-to's." At that time I also spoke concerning the thirty items of the character training. In this message I will not explain them one by one but will only fellowship about them briefly.

Anyone who loves the Lord and is serving the Lord, even if he is not a full-timer, must be built up in his entire person, including areas such as whether one's attire and hairstyle are appropriate and whether one's shoes have been shined. In 1953 I used some wood to build the workers' home across from the meeting hall. It looked simple and crude outside, but it was orderly inside. During the training, when no one was paying attention, I would often go to the workers' home to check how well the tables had been wiped, the beds made, the shoes organized under the beds, and the clothes hung in the closets. It is a pity that later on the co-workers did not practice these matters thoroughly.

Although Mormonism is heretical, the Mormons are more proper and neat than people in Christianity. When the young people among them reach a certain age, they have to render two years of church service. During the service, the boys' hair has to be proper; it cannot be too long. The girls have to be even more proper and dignified. Their schedule is very tight. They do not drink alcohol, tea, or coffee, and they do not smoke. Their practice is successful due to their conduct. Paul told Timothy, "Let no one despise your youth, but be a pattern to the believers in word, in conduct, in love, in faith, in purity"

(1 Tim. 4:12). The conduct mentioned here includes the matter of our clothing and attire being tidy, proper, and dignified.

I do not like to see my co-workers and the full-timers dressed slovenly. The people in Shanghai call these kinds of people "bums." Some people have not polished their shoes for half a year, and their black shoes have become gray shoes. If such a one were to stand before me and speak, I would immediately discredit what he would say by fifty percent, regardless of what he would say. I would not have any confidence in him. One day when I was giving this kind of message about our dress, a brother immediately testified that what I had said was absolutely correct. He said that his father, who is an employer, looks at applicants' shoes when he is interviewing and hiring people. You need to learn in all these matters.

Not only should we dress properly and neatly, even our living place should be clean and tidy both inside and outside. We Chinese are very negligent in this matter. The Japanese clean their dwellings every day. They wipe their tatami once a day. They pay special attention to the four corners of the room and wash the front entrance. The Germans not only wash the steps up to the front porch but also scrub them with soap. It would be considered a great accomplishment if a Chinese family cleaned their house once a week. If you go and examine our meeting hall, you will find that it is very unseemly. There is dust everywhere, yet we do not have any feeling regarding it. The Lord has entrusted so much to us, so how can we allow our meeting hall to be arranged in such a poor way? This is distasteful in the eyes of the unbelievers. We have disgraced ourselves.

Your attire is also often unseemly. Some brothers dress like bums. When they stand up and speak, dressed like a bum, who will listen? I do not have the time today, but if I were to conduct the training myself, the first thing I would do would be to change you thoroughly from head to toe. I am not asking you to buy good clothes. Rather, I want you to dress in a dignified, proper, tidy, and elegant way. You have to admit that if those who work in the bank dressed like you, they would be disqualified. You also have to agree that the church is higher than a bank. The work that we are doing today is much more valuable than the work that is done in a bank. However, the way you look today, you would not be hired, even if you were applying for a job at the bank.

Because of this, I have told you young people many times that you should not acquire the looseness that is among us. I do not like to see you in such a condition, doing things half-heartedly and without enthusiasm, coming to the meetings late, and taking your seats in a disorderly way. As we are learning to serve the Lord, we should be proper, even in the way we walk into a meeting. Do not forget that we are doing a great business for the King of the heavenly kingdom and are representing Him on the earth. Of course, we should not pick up the worldly way. Nevertheless, we need to represent the Lord in a suitable manner.

One time I went to a small group meeting, and a sister told me that she had been touched when she had seen an elderly sister in that meeting who looked graceful and elegant. In my opinion, that elderly sister was very ordinary. She was nothing special. However, when others saw her, they saw a certain kind of expression. This proves that the saints are observing how we who serve the Lord dress and adorn ourselves and how we speak and act. Some of you act very lightly. You swing your arms and shuffle your feet while talking. When you get excited, you push and shove one another like elementary school children. How can you serve the Lord if you behave this way?

Therefore, you also have to learn how to speak. You cannot speak loudly or softly as you like. When you call a hymn in the meeting, your voice must be loud and clear, being considerate of others' ears. If you do not learn to speak with the right volume, speed, and expression, your preaching of the word will be unbearable to others. You also need to learn the proper way to conduct and deport yourself. Do not think that your deportment is unimportant because you have only recently enrolled in the Full-Time Training as a trainee and are nobody important. You are not merely trainees; you are also those who go out to teach people the truth. If you are not properly built up, how can you gain people's respect? In building up yourself, you must pay attention to these small, fine matters.

Consider the matter of attire for example. Some of you are very peculiar in your attire. You wear black shoes with blue socks and brown pants with red ties, which are as far from matching as heaven is from earth. When you stand in front of people and they see you dressed in such a peculiar way, how will they receive your exhortation and teaching? The clothing that you wear is bought with your money, so you should give careful consideration to the clothes that you buy. There is a Chinese saying—"You can tell how things will develop by the small beginning." A person's character is established little by little, just as a house is built by setting small bricks on top of each other one by one. If you do not establish your character in these minor things, it is like building a house with small pieces of bricks that are not uniform in color and shape. The house naturally will not look pleasant or sturdy. Who would want to move into such a house?

I charged you before to thoroughly read and study 1 and 2 Timothy and Titus. Now I would like to ask whether you found all the crucial points concerning fleeing and avoiding in these three books. If you study these points carefully, you will have some understanding regarding this matter of character building. Philippians 4:8 says, "What things are dignified,...what things are well spoken of, if there is any virtue and if any praise, take account of these things." Does your attire and adornment cause others to feel that you are dignified? Does it invite praise? This does not mean that you should pay attention only to one aspect of your character. Rather, you should pay attention to every point and aspect of your character. If you do not take account of these things and do not pay attention to them, then there will be no way for you to build yourself up.

Besides the building up of your character in relation to how you conduct yourself and how you do things, you also need to learn how to carry out the Lord's work. In working for the Lord you need to learn several matters in particular. The first matter is contacting people, the second is ministering the word, and the third is visiting people in their homes or on the campuses. If you learn these few things, you will be quite useful in the Lord's recovery.

THE TRAINING FOR THE CAMPUS WORK

All these points that I have fellowshipped about are areas in which we need to be trained. We must know the way of the Lord's recovery. We need to pursue and enter deeply into the truth. We need to have the experience and growth in life. Furthermore, we need to be built up in the way we conduct ourselves. We must go on from knowing how to conduct ourselves to knowing how to do things, and from knowing how to do things to knowing how to work for the Lord. Regarding the content of the training, I hope that we would be able to coordinate with the campus work in a practical way. I hope that we could have two to three months to be trained to practice how to do a campus work to gain the students. We have much to learn in every aspect in order to handle the need of this work.

Regarding the arrangement of the training schedule, the morning time for pursuing the Word should continue. Another time should be set aside for us to be trained to do the campus work. We all know that every country in the world that does not emphasize education will fall behind. The main reason why Taiwan is prosperous today is that in these years the university students are being educated quite well. Because of this, we must now pay attention to the campuses.

Furthermore, the campus work is also the Lord's flow on the earth today. I have noticed that not only in America and Asia but also in Europe and South America, the college students are very willing to receive the truth, especially the truth in the Bible. Recently in America we sent out gospel teams, with ten people on each team, to the various campuses to take care of the Lord's need. On the campus we do not preach the ordinary gospel but the gospel of the truth. In many places, the first message we give is on the Triune God. This is very attractive in the United States. More than half of the college students in America were born into Christian families. They have already heard many shallow teachings. If we preach the same old teachings, they will feel bored, even though they still desire to know something about God. Therefore, we are eager to publish the New Testament Recovery Version in English to meet this need. Many college students greatly welcomed the New Testament Recovery Version when they saw it.

There is a way and a technique to do things and to work for the Lord. In Philippians 4:12 Paul speaks of the "secret," referring to the key to doing things. Not only do we need the Spirit and the Word in preaching the gospel; we also need the content. Some brothers are strong in their spirit, but the content of their gospel is very light. Therefore, they do not gain many people. The standard of education for the young people has been greatly raised. The young people have their own logic, philosophy, and thinking. The truths in the Lord's Word are very logical and are able to meet the real inner need of people. When we contact the college students on the campuses, the question we must ask is how do we present these logical, high, and rich truths to them in a clear fashion? If we learn the way to contact people and the key in speaking to them, we will be able to touch people in their hearts and gain them right away. Therefore, there is a great deal to learn in this matter.

There are so many of you attending the Full-Time Training. If you go out to work in an ordinary fashion, it will not only be a waste of time but also a waste of your learning. You should cherish the training that you have received to carry out the proper work on the campuses by contacting and gaining the college students. In addition, you must also continue in the basic training and learning. You need to take care of such things as prayer, coordination, fellowship with the Lord, and not being individualistic.

THE BUILDING UP OF OUR HUMAN CHARACTER
BEING THE SECRET

In taking care of practical things and working for the Lord, you do not need to get into the particulars. You simply need to grasp the "secret" and pay attention to being efficient. If you are too particular, you cannot be efficient. Nevertheless, you have to lay hold of the "secret." In order for you to be efficient in doing things and in working, you must first build yourselves up in your human character. Regardless of where I move to, the first thing I do is clean the house thoroughly and then settle down. If you conduct yourselves in a loose way, seeking only for a place to lie down and sleep, this will spoil your character. Not only so, when you work or serve, you will be unprepared and bewildered. This is not acceptable.

Therefore, you need to take this comprehensive message of mine. Do not wait until someone comes to supervise you. Rather, you need to take the initiative to learn here. You have all graduated from college, so you should know what to do. If you learn, practice, and endeavor to build yourselves up in all the points that I have mentioned, the Lord will have a way in you. The urgent need in the Lord's work today is that we would do the campus work to gain the young people for the Lord's recovery that we may have a promising future.

CHAPTER FOUR

THE NEED FOR TRAINING

DIRECTION FOR THOSE CONSIDERING JOINING THE FULL-TIME TRAINING

In Taiwan almost all of the brothers who graduate from college are required to render two years of military service. Thus, if they want to join the training upon graduating, they would have to simultaneously remain in school for another year. Then they would have to prepare for examinations while attending the training and would be unable to focus on the training. Therefore, after graduating from college, many of them do not know whether they should first join the Full-Time Training and then serve in the military or first serve in the military and then join the Full-Time Training. For those of you who are in this situation, this is a practical matter that you must thoroughly consider before the Lord. First, you need to consider whether you will still have the opportunity to be trained after serving in the military for two years. Since the present training in the church is a special training, once you miss this opportunity, you may not have such an opportunity again. If this is the case, then it would be worthwhile to consider deferring the military service to join the training for one year. Otherwise, you should join the military service right after your graduation from college. Nonetheless, this is a personal affair that you yourself must clearly consider. I would suggest that unless there is a special reason, you should do first things first. You should first join the military service to fulfill your obligation and afterward devote yourself wholeheartedly to be trained. Nevertheless, if you feel that your present need is to be trained, then you should grasp this opportunity and consider attending the training for one year.

LEARNING TO BE A PERSON WHO SEIZES THE TIME

Some of the trainees have said that in the training there are too many things to do. They are required to have small groups, to equip themselves with the truth, to pursue life, to preach the gospel, and to learn languages. They also have to go to the campuses to contact, nourish, and take care of people. Therefore, they have asked how they are supposed to manage their time with only twenty-four hours in a day. Furthermore, the training requires them to offer two years to be trained. Afterward, depending on the trainers' observations of them, they may go on to serve full time if they are qualified, or if they are not qualified to serve, they may find a job. Some feel very anxious, not knowing how to make use of the two short years in a serious way that will decide the path that they will take. You may say that the training has too many requirements, but according to my observation, there are actually not that many. It is true that we have only twenty-four hours in a day and that no matter how we use them, we still have only twenty-four hours of time each day. You may feel that the class curriculum is very full and has many requirements, but in my opinion it is not that full. Do not think that only those who are being trained are required to exercise; those who are not being trained also have to exercise in the matters of pursuing to know the truth and growing in life. Concerning the matter of carrying out the group meetings, you do not need to purposely spend time to practice this. Simply devote your whole heart to the meeting when you are there, and endeavor to learn something while doing it. The same principle applies to the campus work. As long as you abide by the schedule, there should not be any problems.

You may feel that the schedule is too busy because you are not used to it. Therefore, you must make a schedule according to the practical situation and abide by it. If you do not make a schedule, time will not wait for you and will pass by very quickly. If you stop to take a few breaths and a rest, your time will be gone. Therefore, you have to learn to grasp the time.

While you are still the master of your time, do your best to learn and practice.

Let me use myself as an example. You are all younger and stronger than I am, yet I do more than you each day. Not only do I have to lead the meetings and visit the churches, I also have to help the literature work. The Living Stream Ministry prints almost two hundred pages of messages per month in English alone, and I am the one who finalizes the manuscripts. Our literature work consists of four lines, one of which is the life-study messages. There are other books for publication that I also need to finalize. In addition, I still have to prepare all the messages for the conferences and trainings, write the truth lessons, and be responsible for the finalization of the Chinese books. If I gave these tasks to someone else, I do not think anyone would be able to do them all. The reason I can do all this is because I have a schedule, and I work according to this schedule.

Hence, you must learn to manage your time and to do things in a logical order. Then you will not feel that the schedule is too full or that you are tired. We human beings are living beings and therefore have a certain degree of flexibility. We can be either too loose or too rigid. Once you set your schedule, even when you relax, you will not be fully relaxed because you will know what step to take next, and you will naturally be ready. However, if you do not have a schedule, you may waste two hours just by being a little bit loose, or you may use up half of your day chatting with people. In the past six months, what has been the result of your pursuit of the truth every morning? How many books have you studied carefully? If you value this matter and set a definite time for your pursuit of the truth, the result will be better than it is at present.

CONSIDERATIONS CONCERNING FULL-TIME SERVICE

You should seriously consider before the Lord whether your full-time service will be short-term or long-term. Perhaps the Lord will give you the feeling that your service should be short-term, in which case you should give two or three years to the Lord, or perhaps the Lord will lead you to serve long-term. Either way, there is a great need for full-time serving ones for the going on of the church.

Currently there are more than eighty elders in the church in Taipei, but only a few of these elders are full-time co-workers serving as elders. Other than the co-workers and the elderly saints, there is not one elder who is serving full time. In other words, elders who are willing to receive a burden, to put aside their worldly future, and to care for the church's needs for the testimony of the Lord have yet to appear. This worries me and grieves me very much, because the church in Taipei, as the largest church on the globe, should be a pattern in many ways to all the churches. Based on Paul's word in 1 Timothy 5, a church that is in a proper condition should have some elders who serve full time. Verse 17 says, "Let the elders who take the lead well be counted worthy of double honor, especially those who labor in word and teaching." Here, the emphasis of the word *honor* is on material supply, referring to the supplying of financial needs. Because some of the elders are full-time serving ones who are taking care of the church and laboring in the word, the saints should supply their material needs. This is an "honor" to them. It is incredible that this kind of situation does not exist in the church in Taipei, which is the largest church. This is truly a great lack in the Lord's recovery.

In the United States the churches began this practice two years ago. At that time I felt that both in the Far East and in America there was a lack of full-time co-workers in the Lord's recovery. I looked to the Lord that He would work in the hearts of the saints and raise up people to receive the burden to serve full time. I had always hoped that in every church there would be at least one full-time serving elder for every fifty people who are meeting. I also had the hope that among the Chinese-speaking saints ten or more would be raised up to be full-time co-workers. Later, I went to the Bay Area for a summer conference and fellowshipped with the brothers regarding this burden. They not only received it but also started to practice it. Almost all of those brothers had gone to the United States for their education. After they graduated, they worked for a period of time. Then for the Lord's work, they quit their jobs to serve the church full time. Presently, the number of full-timers there has increased. Gradually, more elders are serving full time in various places. This is a good sign.

The Mormons have a regulation that requires their young people to do two years of church service. If they do not do this, they lose their membership and cannot take advantage of its benefits. Although we do not offer any such benefits, I hope that the young saints would receive the Lord's leading to voluntarily offer up one to two years after graduating from college to receive the training and to be trained in spiritual matters such as studying the truth, pursuing life, and serving in coordination in the church life. In this way they will lay a good foundation and have a rich deposit within them. Afterward, some may go and get a job, and some may choose to serve full time after it has become manifest that they should do so and have the desire to do so.

I hope you all would realize that what you have faithfully learned in the training will not be in vain. We should not think that after receiving two years of training, those who are qualified will continue to serve full time, and those who are not qualified will be eliminated. In the training, qualification is not an issue, nor is continuing or not continuing to serve. It may become manifest that some should serve full time, yet they may not be able to do so due to their circumstances. Therefore, do not think that after two years of training and after failing the final examination you have no choice but to go back into the world to pick up a job. You must realize that those who serve full time are in the church, and those who have a job in the world are also still in the church.

The two years you have offered for the training will definitely not be wasted because in the training you are studying the truth, pursuing life, exercising to pray much, learning to coordinate in spirit with the brothers and sisters, and learning to serve in the church. If all the young saints could set aside a segment of time for this kind of learning after they graduate from college, this would be a great benefit to them both in the increase of their spiritual deposit and the building up of their character. There is a big difference between someone who has been trained and someone who has not been trained. Therefore, I hope that your decision to attend the training would not be based on whether or not you intend to serve full time permanently. Rather, it should be based on what kind of impact such a basic, spiritual training would have on your life, regardless of whether you end up serving full time or holding a job. Even if you have to hold a job, the two years of training will produce something marvelous in your life.

LEARNING TO MAKE ADJUSTMENTS
AS THE SITUATION DEMANDS AND LEARNING
TO HAVE A FIRM GRASP ON OUR TIME

Some of you may say that making a schedule for contacting people in the training is difficult because unscheduled times of fellowship often interrupt the prearranged activities, making it difficult to follow the schedule. During a person's lifetime, the time when one is a student is the most blessed time because there are not many interruptions. It is a time when one is most able to concentrate on learning. Those who work in offices are there from nine in the morning until five in the evening, so their schedules are also very regular. Hence, if someone who is not a student or does not belong to the working class intends to achieve something, then he must learn how to adapt himself to changing situations. We who serve the Lord are like guerrilla fighters. We must know how to fight using "guerrilla warfare." As soldiers in a conventional army, we will surely be defeated. The army of the church cannot merely be a conventional army fighting a conventional war. The church has to engage in guerrilla warfare, being ready to fight at any time and by any means.

In the past our Chinese hymnals were very disorganized. There were many different hymnals entitled *Hymns 1, Hymns 2, Gospel Hymns, Selected Hymns,* and *Additional Hymns.* As a result, calling hymns in the meetings was quite confusing. Therefore, after the publication of the English hymnal in 1966, we immediately undertook the task of revising the Chinese hymnal. For this task, I translated more than two hundred hymns from English into Chinese. At that time I still had to go to different places in the Far East to carry out my ministry. Therefore, I did most of the translation work on the airplane while I was traveling. Even though I was very busy, I was still able to finish the compilation of the hymnal within one year. Moreover, I completed the job by myself with only a little help from one brother who did the typesetting and proofreading for me.

Today in our work we need to adapt ourselves to changing situations and firmly grasp our time. We cannot do anything and will never accomplish anything unless we have a set schedule. For example, if I had to attend to all the details of my work, I would not finish them even if I had three secretaries helping me. Nearly every day I receive a bundle of letters. There is no way I could reply to all of them one by one. So I have set a principle for myself. I do not read the long letters right away. Rather, I wait until there is more time. If a letter is important, it should not be too long. For example, in a telegram every word counts. If I read every letter that I got, I would not be able to do other things. Many people in the world are waiting to read our books. If I care for only one person by answering his letter, I might lose thousands or tens of thousands of people. In the same principle, you need to learn to decide what to do depending on the situation. In this way you will not feel frustrated.

You also need to learn to overcome your circumstances. Paul said that in all his circumstances, in everything and in all things, he had learned the secret and knew how to conduct himself (Phil. 4:12). You cannot stop learning because you have to attend the meetings, nor can you stop attending the meetings because you have to learn. You should learn to be balanced. You have been learning to serve the Lord for a period of time, so you should be clear that you are engaging in "guerrilla warfare." For example, if you must attend an unscheduled meeting during the time that was originally intended for the pursuit of the Word, then you must make up that time later. If you value the matter of pursuing the Word, you will find some time to make it up. For example, you may get up half an hour early to make up for the time you lost during the week. We all need this kind of attitude.

The young people in Taiwan are full of drive in their

studying, because if they do not study seriously, they most likely will not have a successful future. This is the trend of this age. Therefore, some people sleep for only five hours a day, and their whole family helps them with the other aspects of their life. It would be a tremendous thing if each of you had this kind of attitude. Maybe you could read through all the crucial ministry books in two years. If the co-workers had the attitude of the students in Taiwan, our work would be completely revolutionized and would not be in such a condition today. If you want to have ease and comfort in the Lord's work, you are in the wrong place. There is no ease and comfort in the Lord's work.

THE ONLY WAY BEING
TO VOLUNTARILY CONSECRATE OURSELVES
TO ACTIVELY PURSUE AND LEARN

Someone observed that during the changing of the system I highly regarded the matter of education and edited some teaching materials to meet the need. Therefore, this person asked whether I could likewise prepare a set of teaching materials for the Full-Time Training in order to train different levels of trainees. He also asked whether we could even adopt some of the ways of the theological schools.

First of all, it is not according to the principle in the Bible to establish a school to train people to serve the Lord. In the Old Testament none of the prophets established a school. The prophets sometimes had disciples, but none of those disciples ever became prophets. Apparently, Elisha was Elijah's disciple. In reality, however, Elisha had been chosen by God Himself. In the New Testament age, seminaries began to be established. According to church history, the establishment of seminaries led to professionalism, and once professionalism started, it was easy to bring in commercialism. Many corrupt practices were brought in, and subsequently there were endless struggles for power. The marvelous thing is that although most of those who were greatly used by the Lord throughout the generations did not come out of seminaries, I daresay that there were a few. They came out to serve the Lord not because they had been taught in seminaries, but because they were acting

THE NEED FOR TRAINING

according to the principle of the Nazarite and were taking the way of voluntary consecration. John Wesley, George Whitefield, and Count Zinzendorf, for example, did not have a seminary background.

Actually, because all the saints have occupations, it is not easy to ask everyone to enter into the study of the truth. On the other hand, our preaching of the word in the past has not been very proper. This is why there are the *Truth Lessons* to make up for this. Regarding the Full-Time Training, since you are already putting in twenty-four hours a day, it is not necessarily appropriate to rely on others to instruct and guide you. The most appropriate situation is that you yourself would find a way to learn. In the recovery's sixty years of history, there were many who were rich in truth and had much learning in the matter of life. If you want to learn from the books and seek help from others, you will find a way. This all depends on you. If you do not want to pursue, even the best way will be of no avail to you.

Regarding the church's plan for the training of the saints, the co-workers in the past, being too quiet, did not act aggressively. They should have paid attention to the training earlier and given the young people the help they needed. Nevertheless, this kind of training can meet only a general need; it cannot meet the special need. To meet the special need, there must be a group of believers who would give themselves as Nazarites before the Lord. Therefore, you all need to consecrate yourselves thoroughly and voluntarily and take the initiative to pursue and learn before the Lord. The training can give you only a good, objective environment, including the church life, the rich truths, and the advanced saints who have had experience in both life and service. You need to go further and have a deeper and more solid pursuit by properly utilizing these resources.

DEEPLY PURSUING THE TRUTH

I hope that the co-workers would endeavor to accomplish something and not be so passive, indifferent, and idle as before. George Whitefield was a very powerful preacher because on his knees he pray-read every word and line of

the New Testament in both English and Greek. Thus, the
Bible became a living book to him. When he released a message, he was full of power and authority. If you desire to
accomplish something, you need to be like him in endeavoring
to pursue and to learn. I am famous for being opposed in the
United States. This is probably unprecedented in the history
of Christianity. However, Christianity cannot defeat the
truths that I preach because what the opposers have learned
in the seminaries is so incomplete and limited compared to
what I teach.

Many of the opposers first rose up to attack my teaching
concerning the Triune God. Eventually, however, their mouths
were shut. All they could do was revile me and twist my
words. They were absolutely unable to refute me. I said that
the three of the Divine Trinity are distinct but not separate.
They said, however, that when the Son left the heavens, He
left the Father there, so that when the Son was baptized, the
Father spoke from the heavens. However, in the Gospel of
John, the Lord said many times that He had come from the
Father. The word *from* in Greek is the word *para,* which has
the meaning of "from with." This means that the Lord came
from the Father and with the Father. Not only so, the Lord
also said that the Father was always with Him and that the
Father had not left Him alone (8:16, 29; 16:32). Therefore, the
picture of the Son being baptized in the Jordan River shows
us that the three of the Trinity are distinct. However, we
cannot say that They are separate. No one can deny that
when the Lord Jesus was baptized, He was in the Father, and
the Father was in Him, because the Lord said that the Father
was always with Him.

The truth never has only one side. When expositors grasp
on to one side of the truth and neglect the other sides, this
results in heresy. We do not deny any side of the truth. Rather,
we pay attention to all the sides of the truth. The three of the
Divine Trinity are distinct but not separate. John 10 says that
the Son and the Father are one (v. 30). Chapter seventeen
speaks of the Son lifting up His eyes to heaven to pray to the
Father (v. 1). However, in chapter fourteen, before the Son
prayed to the Father, He said that the Father was in Him and

that He was in the Father (vv. 10-11, 20). People in Christianity cannot comprehend this because they have been influenced by traditional theology and have not carefully studied the text of the Bible.

HAVING AN ACTIVE, AGGRESSIVE ATTITUDE

Therefore, I hope that you would see that although all the truths in the Bible are in our midst, you need to spend time and energy to learn them. This, of course, is not an easy matter. I feel that the co-workers are not aggressive enough and that they should be trained. After I left the Far East in 1961, I did not come back to the Far East to work again. At most I came back to hold conferences and to visit the churches. For more than twenty years I have been living in the Western world, printing English publications in America and sounding out the call for the Lord's recovery. I can proudly tell you that before I went to America there were less than twenty churches in that country. During the past twenty-three years, due to my calling and the publications that I have put out, over three hundred churches have been raised up. The United States and Canada have over one hundred churches, Central and South America have over one hundred churches, and Africa, Europe, and Australia also have over one hundred churches. Before I went abroad, I left the churches in the Far East—the churches in Taiwan in particular—many assets, including a large group of co-workers and a great number of meeting halls. However, during the past twenty years, where has the increase been in Taiwan? At the time I left Taiwan, there were seventy to eighty churches, and now there are not even a hundred. Therefore, I hope that you young saints would learn not to take the old way.

Recently I was in Singapore for a conference of the co-workers from the Far East. Co-workers from Thailand, Singapore, Malaysia, and Indonesia attended. One day I openly rebuked some of the co-workers. I was not opposing them. I was supporting them, but within me there was a feeling of indignation. I wish that, as Paul said, I could provoke them to jealousy (Rom. 11:14) so that they would rise up and hate themselves and not be so loose anymore. I wish that in continuing to work, they would have the determination to produce results, even if they have to hit their heads against the wall. Otherwise, they should discontinue their work and find a proper job. Instead of always "occupying the nest without laying any eggs," they should let the young people try to produce some results. I do not trust in the old way. Even I am taking the lead to try new things and to make changes.

Every word in the footnotes of the New Testament Recovery Version was written by me. Every time I go back to read those footnotes, I marvel at how I could have written such words that are full of light, revelation, and supply. I am not being proud. In my hometown of Chefoo during the summer of 1936, eleven years after I was saved, I wrote two pamphlets called *Gleanings from the Genealogy of Christ* and *Gleanings of the Generations*. Even today it is hard to find a book among all the books published by Christianity on the genealogy of Christ that can be compared to *Gleanings from the Genealogy of Christ*. I accomplished these things altogether by my personal learning day by day during the past sixty years. Some people say that I can do so much because I have an inborn talent and am a smart learner. Actually, I do not have as much natural talent as you. The only advantage I may have over you is that I am fond of studying and can study tirelessly. Today, regardless of what I am writing, I still consult the dictionaries often to study the meanings of words.

I do not think that you have exhausted all your energy, nor have you spent your energy in a proper way. If I were conducting the training, your days would be different than they are now. You would probably feel that no day is good. You have not truly experienced hardship. Thus, when the schedule is somewhat busy, you feel that it is unbearable. I do not like to hear the brothers say, "This is too stressful. We cannot bear it." If you truly cannot bear it, then how is it that you can still eat and sleep well? The fact that you can still eat and sleep well proves that you are still living comfortably. You truly need to be constricted.

Some say that being a co-worker in the recovery is like having a secure job, because once you have been recognized as a co-worker, you are a co-worker for your whole life. There is no need to be tested or evaluated. If there were testing, our situation would not be as it is today. However, once there is testing, the matter of working for the Lord becomes professionalized. This is something that we do not want to see. I began conducting the training in 1953. Looking back, I am not satisfied with that training. After much inward consideration, I would like to completely change my way this time. First I will give you a demonstration, a pattern. Then I hope that I can change your concept and stir you up to endeavor.

Do not always expect others to teach you. Rather, you need to pursue deeply and diligently on your own. I did not read many books when I was young, and Christianity at that time was not publishing any books of value. Between 1936 and 1939 Brother Nee purposely did not publish any books because he wanted to see what Christianity could produce. Under those circumstances, I still endeavored to learn. Therefore, you need to be stirred up. When I was conducting the training in 1953, I told the trainees that when I was in elementary school, I read a proverb that said that if your handwriting is poor, you should not blame the pen or the ink but yourself for your lack of practice. Similarly, you should not complain about the environment or other matters. Rather, you should blame yourself for not laboring enough.

The current situation is exceedingly favorable to you, but you are taking all the blessings for granted. Consider the church life for example. When I got saved, I was young, and there was no church life. The church life in Shanghai in 1940 was nothing like today's church life. At that time, we pursued the few books that Brother Nee had published. We not only read them, we read them many times. I started to use the Interlinear Greek-English New Testament in the winter of 1932. No one ever taught me Greek. I learned the words and the grammar entirely on my own. As the saying goes, "Rome was not built in a day." Even though I could not understand Greek, I toiled, spending much time and energy to get deeply into my studies. For example, the Greek word for *truth* is *aletheia*. There are eight denotations of this word in the New Testament. Footnote 6 of 1 John 1:6 explains this very clearly.

Even a Greek expert probably could not give such a complete explanation of this point.

RADICALLY CHANGING OUR CHARACTER

I am speaking these things to stimulate you so that you would stop thinking about getting help from theological seminaries. A theological seminary can teach you only to be a man with mediocre ability. If you want to be only a man with mediocre ability, then you may go to a seminary to be taught. In the training there is an ideal environment in which you can learn. Even if you eventually get a secular job and do not become a full-time serving one, the learning and influence you receive during these two years will benefit you. What I regret the most is the pitiful condition of those of us who are Chinese and who have entered into the church. I am not saying that the church is not good. The church is good, but man's condition is not good. You have brought all the bad things of the Chinese culture into the church, such as looseness of character, lack of vitality, disorder in the meetings, and a lack of tidiness and neatness in the meeting hall. I have been groaning unceasingly about this situation. I simply cannot imagine that the elders and co-workers could lead the churches into such a situation. We are not keeping up with the times.

I am not telling you to be rebellious or to nullify everything that the co-workers have done in the past and to depreciate them. Praise the Lord that they have done their part. However, their character is undesirable. In this matter you should not learn from them. There was a great entrepreneur in Taiwan whose success was the issue of his own hard work. He said, "We all say that Japan's economy is good, but why are we unwilling to learn from them?" This person was right. We should learn to have the spirit of the Japanese. Regarding the publication work, Japan is the best, the United States is second, and Taiwan is third. The printing press for the Japanese bookroom is in a small, square room directly above the meeting hall and is much smaller than Taiwan's printing press, yet Taiwan's products cannot match the standard of the products put out by the Japanese saints.

For another example, consider the carrying out of the video trainings. The church in Tokyo abides by all the regulations of the video training. The churches in Taiwan, however, violate many of the regulations. Every locality is required to keep an attendance record of the video training and to send a report to the ministry station. Only the church in Tokyo sends a report that is neat and clean; the report from Taiwan is altogether unclear. Not only so, in order that those attending the training would have some sense of responsibility and in order to raise the standard of the training, those attending the training are required to make a donation. Again, the church in Tokyo does an accurate job in this matter. Their accounts are very clear and orderly with no mistakes. The most disorderly accounts are from Taiwan.

When we do things in a serious way, results will be produced, and we will make progress. The social trend, tradition, and natural habit of the Chinese people, all of which are in our blood, are altogether the opposite. Therefore, when you learn to do the Lord's work, the first thing you must do is to have a radical change in your character. You must completely change the Chinese character that is within you. If you learn to do this within two years, then you would be the best in whatever you do, even if you take a secular job. However, if you refuse to change your character, then you will be of little use, no matter what you do.

CHAPTER FIVE

BUILDING UP THE CHARACTER OF THE LORD'S SERVING ONES

THE NEED TO BE STRICT IN THE FULL-TIME TRAINING

We need to be strict in this term of the Full-Time Training. For twenty years we have suffered damage because the training has not been strict enough. This time I hope that we would have a completely new and strict beginning in the training. Anyone who has ever served in the military knows that once a person joins the military, he loses all his freedom. All his exercises and activities are directed by a single word of command. He is thoroughly changed from head to toe so that he may be freshly equipped to receive strict military training. Without rigorous training, an army cannot fight a battle. No looseness is allowed, because the improper conduct of one person during a battle could lead to the destruction of the whole army.

I asked you to thoroughly study the three books of 1 Timothy, 2 Timothy, and Titus before coming to the training. In 2 Timothy 2:3-4, Paul told Timothy, "Suffer evil with me as a good soldier of Christ Jesus. No one serving as a soldier entangles himself with the affairs of this life, that he may please the one who enlisted him." Verse 4 clearly points out that the primary matter for a soldier is that he must not entangle himself with the affairs of this life.

Every contestant who runs on a racecourse does his best to dress as simply as possible. He does not want to bear any excess weight that can become an entanglement to him during the race. This makes it easier for him to finish the race and receive the crown. Similarly, in order to win a battle, a soldier must not allow himself to be entangled with the affairs and burdens of this life. Since you have come to the training, you must hold the same kind of attitude as that of an athlete running on a racecourse and a soldier fighting on a battlefield. If you do not have this kind of spirit, I would urge you to go back to your job.

In the world, people can relax after completing their military service. However, as good soldiers serving the Lord in the church, we have been enlisted not merely for two years of preparatory service but for a lifetime of service. Therefore, do not think that you can relax after graduating from two years of training. Remember, you must be a good soldier for your entire life. From now on you must all have such a spirit. You must make a determination before the Lord, saying, "Lord, I am joining Your army to be a good soldier for my whole life." First Peter 4:1 says that we should arm ourselves with a mind to suffer. Every soldier expects hardship. No one serving as a soldier expects a life of pleasure.

THE IMPORTANCE OF CHARACTER

In 1953 we held a training in Taipei that was very strict at the time. Later, however, I was troubled, because in my view none of those who were in that training had become useful. The primary reason was that they failed to build up a proper character. The work of the Lord's recovery in the Far East has been greatly frustrated mainly because of the Chinese character.

The Lord has been quite merciful in giving the Chinese people very intelligent minds. The whole world recognizes the intelligence of the Jews. However, according to what I have observed in the United States over the years, the minds of the Jews are not necessarily sharper than those of the Chinese. No one can deny, though, that the Jews are firm in their will and strong in their determination. This is the secret of their success. Once they decide on a matter, they will press on resolutely and will not give up until they reach their goal. This is the life-pulse that enables them to stand. Secondly, the Jews are very enterprising and diligent. For much of the past two thousand years, the Jews were without a nation. This was a suffering to them, and they wandered from place to place.

They were rejected and persecuted by the entire world, especially during World War II when millions of them were massacred by Hitler. However, because of their diligence and endeavoring, they have reached the peak in their attainments in the United States and have become the focus of the world.

The Chinese people in America today are the same. The reason they are successful is because they are smart, enterprising, diligent, and determined. Even though there are laws in the United States that protect minorities from discrimination, in actuality, minorities are not that protected. This compels the Chinese students who study in America to make even more of an effort to succeed. If it were not for this situation, it would be difficult for them to succeed. The Jews are successful because of their determination and diligence. The Chinese are smart but lack determination. Those Chinese students who study abroad are successful because they are compelled to be determined and diligent. However, if they were to stay in their own country, they would readily become loose and lazy under the influence of the environment. A major weakness of the Chinese character is that Chinese people do not strive to improve unless they are forced and pressed by the circumstances to improve.

POOR CHARACTER BEING
A HINDRANCE TO THE LORD'S WORK

The reason the Lord's work in Taiwan has been frustrated and has not been spreading is that for the past twenty years the churches here have been living a life of ease and comfort. When I left Taiwan in 1961, there was a great number of saints meeting in the church in Taipei. Since then, however, not only has there been a lack of expansion, but there has even been a decrease. The reason lies in the fact that the church in Taipei has many assets and a great number of saints in the meetings, so the co-workers have been able to maintain the situation without having to endeavor and struggle for the spread of the work. In other words, when I left, I left the church in Taipei with many assets. This allowed the co-workers to quickly become loose.

On the one hand, I can testify that the co-workers have

faithfully maintained the testimony of the Lord's recovery in Taiwan. On the other hand, during the past twenty or more years, all the shortcomings of the Chinese character were brought into the church because of their carelessness and inattentiveness. Since there are so many valuable assets in the church, they tend not to care when they lose a few of the saints. They may feel that the absence of these saints does not make much of a difference and that there are still thousands of people who attend the conferences. However, as the saying goes, "One false step makes a great difference." During the past twenty-five years, not only has the number of saints in the meetings decreased, but even the spirit for expansion which was among us has been lost.

The work of the Lord's recovery in Taiwan began at the site of Hall 1 of the church in Taipei, which was part of a Japanese residential district during the Japanese occupation. That area was bombed by the allied forces during the war, and all that was left was an area of cement-covered ground. After the victory, this plot of land was taken over by the Chinese government. Later two Chinese brothers who had been living overseas came to reside in Taiwan and bought half of the land. Eventually, a small meeting hall that could accommodate three to four hundred people was built. On August 1, 1949, I held our first conference in that little meeting hall to officially start the Lord's work in Taiwan.

After the beginning of the work, under the Lord's blessing the number of saved ones steadily increased. As a result, our meeting place quickly became inadequate. In 1950 we made use of the adjacent empty lot by fixing it up and putting a bamboo fence around it. Thus, we were able to add many more seats to the hall. Later as the Lord's work spread more, and the number of saints multiplied, I bought another piece of land next to the meeting hall, combining it with the land that we originally owned, and we rebuilt the meeting hall.

In 1953 I began to conduct a training which many saints attended. On the fenced lot I built a house for the workers. Even though its appearance was simple, the lush plants and flowers provided a sense of serenity and freshness, and its interior was clean and tidy. I left Taiwan in 1961 and did not come back until 1965. When I came back, the workers' house was almost unrecognizable. The plants had dried up, and all the flowers had withered. Everything was a mess. I was exceedingly troubled within. I thought back to when I had conducted the training twelve years earlier and had spoken on the thirty items of character training. The messages that I had given at that time had been very strong and serious, yet twelve years later, the co-workers had completely forgotten them.

Recently I told the elders that our meeting hall, which is now a building made of reinforced concrete, is no longer the simple building we once had. Therefore, it should not have an old appearance. Regarding the condition of the meeting hall, if the hall were being used by the Japanese saints, it would definitely be tidier and cleaner than it is today. If it were being used by the American saints, it would be much more spacious and elegant. However, when we use the meeting hall, we make it appear so unbecoming. For example, consider the bookshelves which contain the Bibles and hymnals for public use. All of the Bibles and hymnals are in disarray, and many of them are torn and are even missing pages. Not one of them is in a proper condition. This implies that our work has not been developed and has no vitality. If people came and saw the disorderly condition of our Bibles and hymnals, how could they respect us?

In this world every building, regardless of what kind of business it is used for, needs to have an impressive front. For example, the people who work at a bank must clean their surroundings so that everything is neat and tidy. When people see that the bank's environment is respectable, then they are more likely to have confidence in the bank and to be willing to deposit their money there. Similarly, every week we should organize the books and hymnals on our bookshelves that are for public use. The torn ones should be repaired, and the ones that are no longer usable should be replaced. The books should be neatly placed on the shelf so that in the next meeting they can be properly distributed. Do not look down on these kinds of matters. A little bookshelf could ruin our reputation, resulting in our being unable to bring in anyone of quality, or it could be our silent testimony, attracting people to us. Therefore, as we are working here, we should have an impressive front, a dignified appearance, so that people would be fully convinced to come to us.

Please forgive me for saying these things. I must say them because I hate how the Chinese character has damaged us. There are many business entrepreneurs in Taiwan who are successful because they have changed their character. As long as one is willing to change his poor character, he will ultimately succeed. Those who do not change their slothful nature will fail. Those who change the fastest, the earliest, and the most radically will have the greatest chance of success.

THE SUCCESS OF THE CHURCH SERVICE DEPENDING ON THE BUILDING UP OF A PROPER CHARACTER

Serving in the church is similar to opening a restaurant. Suppose someone sets up a food stand on the side of the road by putting out a table and a few chairs, while someone else opens a very respectable restaurant by spending a large amount of money on furnishings and decoration. The two restaurants are alike in that they will both get customers, but the difference is that they will get different kinds of customers. It is the same with the church. If we are rough in the way we handle the services in the church, then it will be hard to gain people of high quality. Of course, this does not mean that we despise people of low quality, because it is possible for someone who is a "small potato" to be gained by the Lord and to become a "V.I.P." Nevertheless, we still hope that many capable, promising, and reputable people would be brought into the church. For this reason we should carefully reexamine and reconsider our present way of service.

Even though our work has not produced any obvious results in the past years, we are still holding to the truth clearly and firmly, and the elders and co-workers among us have also been increasingly equipped in life. These two matters are truly the most precious aspects of our inheritance, and you should pay attention to them. However, you may have learned the truth and grown in life, but if the standard of your conduct and work is low and if your character is still loose, then your service in the church will surely be ineffective.

For example, consider a scholar. A scholar may be very knowledgeable, but if while he is teaching, he wears shabby clothes and his character is very sloppy, then he will not produce good students. He must have a proper character in his conduct and work. An ancient Chinese sage once said that in order to govern a nation, one must first be able to manage his own family, and in order to manage one's own family, one must first be able to cultivate himself. You must first perfect your character, be regular in your living and activities, and maintain a clean and elegant environment. Only then will it be possible for you to succeed in your career. Therefore, we have to treasure the life and the truth in the recovery, but we cannot continue to be loose in our character.

HAVING A GOOD CHARACTER
TO MEET THE LORD'S NEED IN THIS AGE

We all need to realize that the age we are in is an age of aggressive competition. There is competition among countries, among people, and among different occupations and businesses. There is competition everywhere. American professors have a motto that says, "Publish or perish." In other words, if you are a professor and do not produce any articles for publication within a certain amount of time, you will be eliminated. I hope that you would all be stirred up to repent of your loose character and to make a change in your character.

I am not criticizing you for being lazy, but I suspect that you have been affected by tradition. You are proud and contented and not humble or diligent enough. This has caused other Christian groups to surpass us. There is a group in Korea, for example, that started in 1958 with only three couples meeting together. At that time, we already had thousands of saints in Taipei. Yet today that group has a few hundred thousand members in Seoul alone, while we are contented and satisfied with our situation and remain behind our closed doors.

THE DILIGENCE OF OUR CHARACTER
AFFECTING THE LORD'S WORK

For all of the reasons that I have given above, I feel that the training in the past was a big failure. If I had more time and energy, I would use five or six months to train you day after day as I did thirty years ago. However, this time we have only three months. The truths in the recovery will always remain with us, and life will be a matter that we will always need. For the past sixty years, these two items have been the precious inheritance of those in the Lord's recovery. Therefore, we must guard them securely. However, we must also remember that in everything we do, we will either keep progressing or fall behind. If we continue to be at ease, content, and loose, then those behind us will catch up to us and leave us far behind.

I hope the fellowship that I am giving you would not go in one ear and out the other. If you do not pay attention to your character from the very beginning, then everything that you learn regarding the full-time service will be worthless. I am here because when I was young, I realized and concluded that serving the Lord full time was the highest and best way to live the human life. For this, I risked and offered up my entire life. Although I have flaws and shortcomings, by the Lord's mercy, I have been faithful to my consecration and to this day am still striving to be faithful. I rise up every morning at 5:45 and get washed up. Then I start to work. This morning, before you got up, I was already reading manuscripts and writing letters. In my collection of books, I have a great number of dictionaries, which I use frequently. Not only so, when better dictionaries or concordances are published, I buy them immediately, whether they are in Chinese, English, or Greek. I hope that you would learn from me in all these matters and not only be diligent but exceptionally diligent.

Second Timothy mentions three important matters: pursuing the truth, growing in life, and being diligent. You cannot read these things and then quickly disregard them. Paul told Timothy, "Be diligent to present yourself approved to God, an unashamed workman, cutting straight the word of the truth" (2:15). Cutting straight the word of the truth cannot be accomplished by casually reading the Bible. Rather, you need to study the truth in depth. For example, a surgeon needs to develop good surgical skills in order to be a good surgeon. He needs to study the human body in depth and to practice doing surgery many times. In the same way, if you are going to cut straight the word of the truth, you need to spend time and energy to get into the truth. This cannot be accomplished in one or two days.

EXERCISING OURSELVES IN WORD AND CONDUCT AND NOT LETTING OTHERS DESPISE OUR YOUTH

If you study the footnotes in the New Testament Recovery Version, you will discover that those footnotes were not composed in a loose way. I revised the footnotes repeatedly until they accurately expressed the meaning of the truth. To study in Taiwan you need to strive and to be industrious. Our striving and being industrious are related to our character. What Paul said to Timothy was entirely related to the matter of character. Perhaps you may say that although the letters to Timothy mention many matters, the word *character* is never mentioned. This is correct. However, the charge that Paul gave to Timothy was definitely a teaching regarding the matter of character.

In 1 Timothy 4:12 Paul said to Timothy, "Let no one despise your youth, but be a pattern to the believers in word, in conduct, in love, in faith, in purity." This verse has a very profound meaning. You should not let anyone despise your youth. However, if your attire is unsuitable and your speech is inappropriate, how could others not despise your youth? If you are careless and frivolous in your actions, people will spontaneously despise your youth. Therefore, what Paul was telling Timothy in this verse was that Timothy should be dignified in his conduct and actions and proper in his speech. What he said, how much he said, and when and how he said things should have caused others to respect him rather than despise his youth.

In this verse Paul first mentioned our words, then our conduct, behavior, and actions, and lastly our love, faith, and purity. Love and faith are matters of life, whereas our words and conduct are matters of our character. If we were to write this verse, we would mention faith and love first and then conduct and word. However, in doing so we would mistake the means for the end and say exactly the opposite of what Paul said.

I do not intend to boast, but I would like to testify that when I was thirty-one years old, I was already pursuing the truth. One day a brother said to me, "Brother Lee, I would like to know what your background is, because you seem to be someone of noble birth in your words, actions, conduct, and manner of speech." I answered, "My background is not noble but poor. When I was ten and was beginning to understand the affairs of human life, I realized that my family was in a destitute situation." I was of a lowborn family, but I was strict regarding my education. Thus, as one who was still in school, whenever I stood up to speak, people around me, including the elderly, would become quiet and respectfully listen to my speaking.

Wherever I go in the United States, those who have a higher status than I still respect me, even though I am Chinese. If I seemed like a lower class person, they would not respect me, and it would be difficult for them to accept my speaking, no matter how well I could speak. Thus, in order that others would not despise your youth, you should learn of me and be strict from your youth in disciplining yourself and taking the initiative to learn by yourself.

In the recovery we emphasize the way of life. The way of life is not a matter of ethics, morality, or culture but a matter of walking according to the Spirit. In light of this, some may say that character training is contrary to our emphasis in the recovery. They may say that character training is not a matter of life but a matter of developing our "bright virtue." However, surely the character of a person who walks according to the Spirit would be much higher than the character of a person who develops his bright virtue. If we talk about life, but our character is lower than the character of those who develop their bright virtue, then we make the salvation of the Lord Jesus worthless. I hate for this to happen. In the recovery we are pursuing the truth, we are learning to take the way of life, and we are proper with regard to morality. However, when we examine the matter of our human character, immediately our inadequate condition is exposed. We are lacking in diligence and seriousness, and we are short in pursuing, making progress, and learning. This makes me very sorrowful.

A DISCIPLINED CHARACTER
BEING NECESSARY FOR PROGRESS
IN THE LORD'S WORK

Because of our shortages with regard to character, the church is not highly respected in people's eyes. Our way of working is not very high, so when a Christian group with a way that is superior to ours emerges, we immediately fall behind. Thirty-five years ago in the Far East, there were not many groups that had as many high quality people as we had in the Lord's recovery. When we were in mainland China, a group of saints was raised up among us. When we officially began the work in Taiwan on August 1, 1949, we had only four to five hundred brothers and sisters on the island of Taiwan and a little over a hundred in Taipei. In 1955, after six years, there were 45,000 believers in the churches on the entire island. Other groups could not match our large size. However, today these groups have adopted a number of our ways and even improved on them through further study and revision. We have the truth and life, but because we have been so closed to new things and have confined ourselves to the old ways, we have fallen behind the other groups.

For example, some Christian groups are now using small groups to bring hundreds and thousands of people to salvation. Thirty years ago we already had the practice of the small groups. We used the small groups as a means of going from house to house to bring people to salvation. However, we unconsciously dropped the practice of the small groups and started to bring people to the meeting hall to gather them for conferences. Outwardly, the conferences seemed to be merely conferences, but in reality they had become occasions for "celebrity speeches." This may be likened to gathering students to a school that does not have classes, classrooms, or teachers but only a few celebrities who come in to speak, and hoping that the students will eventually be able to graduate after hearing this kind of speaking for ten years. Our work in the past replaced the cause with the effect. Speeches display a person's achievements, but if you want to learn the way to attain to those achievements yourself, you need to go through certain courses and learn them sequentially, lesson by lesson.

THE DEGREE OF OUR PURSUIT OF THE TRUTH AND LEARNING IN LIFE DEPENDING ON THE EXTENT OF OUR CHARACTER TRAINING

It is good that in the recovery we have truth and life. We have these items, but we have not entered into them to a very high degree. Therefore, I hope that in this training you would be faithful to build up your character. You should not be loose in the way you conduct yourself, in the way you do things. Instead, you must be diligent, you must learn, and you must make progress. In this training our emphasis is not on the teaching of the truth. We are only asking you to diligently study the New Testament Recovery Version and the life-study messages. Since we have an abundance of spiritual literature among us, our classes will be taught in a way similar to the way graduate classes are taught. This means that we will give you only the necessary directions and guidelines. The most important matter in this training is that in your pursuit of life you would endeavor to change your character to a character that is strict and not loose in any way. This will play a big part in determining whether or not you will be useful to the Lord in the future.

Character building is related to the habits that we acquire. We may even say that character is largely composed of acquired habits. Whereas nature is an inward matter, character is an outward matter. Seventy percent of a person's character is acquired by building, and thirty percent is acquired by birth. Beginning today you need to have a change in your concepts concerning everything great and small. You need to have a set time to rise up, a set time to pray, a set time to read the Word, and a set time to study. Everything must have a set time. You must be strict in practicing these points, not allowing yourself to become loose.

DOING, LEARNING, AND STUDYING SIMULTANEOUSLY

Moreover, you also need to exert an effort to learn several languages. In order to work for the Lord, you must be able to cut straight the word of the truth. You have to get into the depths of the truth to study it. However, if you are not fluent in certain languages, you will have no way to get into the depths of the truth. If you were illiterate, you would be unable to read anything, not to mention the Bible, and would naturally be unable to study the truth. Today it is very common for people to communicate with others all over the world. The environment around the whole world is one of openness and circulation. English is the international language and the one that is most commonly spoken. A great number of spiritual books and magazines have been made available to the public in English. If you want to serve the Lord, it is not sufficient to be skillful only in your own native language. You must also understand English, which is the most widely used language.

The text of the New Testament was originally written in Greek. Since the source of the truth lies in the New Testament, you must also learn Greek. At least you have to learn the Greek alphabet, be familiar with Greek grammar, and be able to use reference books. As you are working for the Lord, you have to speak for Him. Speaking is intimately related to language. Your manner of speaking exposes how much you have studied. Therefore, you need to read many books and endeavor to learn some languages.

I regret that I did not learn enough. If I were still your age, I would learn at least ten more languages. I truly hope that you would work, learn, and study at the same time. You should get a good dictionary and reference book and seriously study them every day. Do not study too many things at once. Simply spend your time and energy in an earnest way on a few of them. In the winter of 1932, I began learning to use the Interlinear Greek-English New Testament. The copy I used then is still in my possession. I hope that you would all do the same, studying in a serious way and making your time in the Full-Time Training worthwhile and meaningful. Otherwise, you will be wasting your time in the training.

CHARACTER BEING THE LIFE-PULSE OF SERVICE

The character that you build up during the training has to become your habit and eventually your daily life. No matter how busy I am in my daily life, I make my bed when I get up every day, unless my wife voluntarily does it for me. After I change, I do not place my clothes in random places. I always place them neatly in specific places. Sometimes when I get up in the middle of the night, I do not even need to turn on the light to find my clothes. I can reach out my hand and know exactly where they are. Character depends wholly on our continual exercise to develop the habits of our daily living. If you cannot even set your clothes straight, how can you cut straight the word of the truth? Your ability to cut straight the word of the truth depends on whether or not you have built up your character. These two matters are very much related to one another.

Our bedrooms should be clean and neat. We should have a habit of cleanliness. Cleanliness is the characteristic that the Chinese culture lacks the most. You cannot say that it does not matter if your bedroom is a mess, it is all right since the main purpose of a bedroom is to have a place to sleep. You must remember that when your room is in order, then your preaching will be orderly, your work will be orderly, and your leading of the church will also be orderly. If your room looks improper, then when you manage the church affairs, you will make a mess of them as well. I am not saying that you need to decorate your room in an excessive, wasteful, or particular manner. I am saying that since you are a human being and not a beast, you should have a decent living place. If possible, you should obtain flowers and plants to help uplift your spirit.

Today I have been forced to say such a strong word. Though I conducted trainings in the past, I did not see any changes in those whom I trained. Today I am repeating the commandments to you, the younger generation. Those who were before you are a generation older than you. In morality, life, and many other aspects, they are your good examples. However, you should not pick up their character and way of serving. If you do, your future, education, business, and occupation will all be a failure, and our work will not be accomplished.

I am not speaking in this way to cause you to rebel against the older generation. Rather, I hope that you would have a change in character. Although you are not in the military, we still hope that this new beginning would be somewhat militaristic. In the matter of attire you should exercise not to be wasteful but to be clean, neat, and dignified, so that when you go out, you will have a proper appearance. Your living quarters should be arranged in a clean, simple, plain, and elegant way. Otherwise, you will not be qualified to be trained here. I hope you all are clear regarding the principles set forth here.

CHAPTER SIX

TRAINING OUR CHARACTER
IN COOPERATION WITH THE LORD

KNOWING THE CRUCIAL POINTS OF THE REVELATIONS AND TEACHINGS IN THE SCRIPTURES

During the past sixty years, the trainings that we have held have been focused on four matters—truth, life, the gospel, and either service or the church, which are two aspects of one thing. All the revelations and teachings in the New Testament may be summed up in these four matters.

The way in which the Bible was written is not like the systematized way in which today's theology is composed. There is nothing systematized or categorized about the Old and New Testaments. Although we have grouped the crucial points of the New Testament into the four categories of truth, life, the gospel, and service, the New Testament itself is not categorized in this way. The New Testament covers a great variety of subjects, and these subjects are scattered throughout the New Testament. For example, although the subject of the Gospel of Matthew is not the church, Matthew 16 and 18 contain a great revelation concerning the church. Matthew 16:18 says, "Upon this rock I will build My church, and the gates of Hades shall not prevail against it," and 18:17 says, "And if he refuses to hear them, tell it to the church; and if he refuses to hear the church also, let him be to you just like the Gentile and the tax collector." In the New Testament all the revelations from Acts to Revelation that pertain to the church are developed according to these two simple verses. This shows us that the New Testament was not written in a systematized or categorized way but in a scattered way—one point is here and another point is there.

Most Bible scholars cannot explain why God wrote the Bible in such a way. According to our way of thinking, the Bible would have been easier to understand if it had been categorized and organized into a system similar to today's systematic theology. We may think that the New Testament would be better if it were composed of only five chapters—chapter one on the truth, chapter two on life, chapter three on the gospel, chapter four on service, and chapter five on the church. If this were the case, taking a Bible class would be as easy as taking a secular class. However, the New Testament was not written in a systematized or categorized way. If you do not read the twenty-seven books of the New Testament carefully, and if you have no desire to progress or advance in your study of the Bible, then you will have no clue as to the meaning of the Bible and will not realize what it says.

In Matthew 16 the Lord Jesus did not say, "Today let us go into the region of Caesarea Philippi. There the sky is clear, and I can sit down and speak to you about the matter of the church." He did not do this. Instead, He simply asked them, "Who do you say that I am?" Peter answered and said, "You are the Christ, the Son of the living God." Then the Lord said, "Flesh and blood has not revealed this to you, but My Father who is in the heavens. And I also say to you that you are Peter, and upon this rock I will build My church" (vv. 15-18). After speaking these things He showed His disciples that He must go to Jerusalem, suffer many things, be killed, and on the third day be raised. Upon hearing this Peter said, "God be merciful to You, Lord! This shall by no means happen to You!" But the Lord turned and said to him, "Get behind Me, Satan!" Then the Lord told His disciples that they must follow Him by taking the way of the cross (vv. 21-24). The Lord first spoke about the church, then He mentioned Satan, and finally He referred to the way of the cross. Since this is the way that the Bible was written, we must consider what the best way to read it is.

The matter of life is also not presented in the Bible in a systematic way. It would not be very easy for someone who has been a believer for only a short time to find the line of life in the Scriptures. Perhaps we in the recovery do not even know where the word *life* is first mentioned in the New Testament. This shows us that in reading the Bible we truly need to be skillful.

The first time the Chinese version of the New Testament mentions the word *life* is in Matthew 6:25, which says, "I say to you, Do not be anxious for your life." In the first five chapters of Matthew there is no mention of the word *life*. Matthew 1, a chapter on the genealogy of Christ, uses the word *begot*, a verb that means "to generate life." Chapter two speaks of King Herod's intention to seek the Lord Jesus and destroy Him. In this chapter there is only killing; there is no life. Chapter three contains the message that John the Baptist preached in the wilderness, in which he told people to produce fruit worthy of their repentance. This is not an explanation of life. Chapter four speaks of the Lord Jesus' being tempted and His calling of the four disciples. First, He told the devil, "Man shall not live on bread alone" (v. 4). The word *live* is in this verse but not the word *life*. Later when He called His disciples, He was like "a great light" (v. 16). Although John 1:4 tells us that "the life was the light of men," Matthew 4 does not mention life in conjunction with light. Hence, in reading the Bible we need a proper mind. On the one hand, we must be able to uncover all the implications of a certain word, such as the word *life,* but on the other hand, we must uncover the revelation of life that is presented in plain words in the New Testament and not extend the meaning of any word in a careless way.

Although we now know that the first mention of the word *life* in the Chinese version of the New Testament is in Matthew 6, we still have to find out what kind of life is referred to here. The New Testament mentions three kinds of life. The first kind of life is the physical life. The Greek word for this kind of life is *bios,* which is the root of the English word *biology.* Another kind of life is the soul-life. The Greek word for this kind of life is *psuche,* which refers to our natural life. The third kind of life is the eternal life, and the Greek word for this life is *zoe.* This is the life that we receive into our spirit from God. The word *zoe* does not appear in the New Testament until Matthew 7:14. It is frequently used in speaking of spiritual matters. Generally speaking, what we eat, what we drink, and what we wear are matters that are primarily related to our physical life. However, although the word *life* in Matthew 6:25 is used in relation to our physical eating and drinking, the word *anxious* in this verse indicates that in this verse life is related to the soul. The word *life* in this verse is literally the word *soul,* referring to the soul-life, in which the desire and appetite for food and clothing reside.

READING THE WORD AND ENTERING INTO IT REQUIRING US TO BE CAREFUL, TO BE SKILLFUL, AND TO EXERT EFFORT

I have given you these examples to show you that reading the Bible is not a simple matter. Since our training is based on the four aspects of the revelation in the New Testament—truth, life, the gospel, and service (or the church)—I hope that you all would exert an effort to read the life-study messages and footnotes according to the sequence of the New Testament. If you do this, you will be powerful in preaching the gospel. If someone asks you a question, you will be able to answer him right away. Those who know that you are serving full time may think that you are a Bible expert, so if you are unable to immediately answer their questions and have to go back to study the Bible in order to do so, they will be disheartened, and you will not have as much impact with them. However, if you are able to quote the Scriptures and give a brief explanation, they will be interested in listening to you, and it will be easy for you to gain them. This has much to do with the extent of your scholastic pursuit and personal study.

In 1943 I was laboring in Chefoo. At that time Chefoo was under the occupation of the Japanese. The church did not have a denominational background and there were no Western missionaries in it, yet our work brought in a big revival. The number of people meeting with us at that time was greater than the total number in the eight local denominations raised up by the missionaries. Almost every one of us sold everything and gave all that we had to the church. Seventy saints migrated to Suiyüan Province, and thirty moved to the mouth of the Sungari River. Because of this, the

Japanese secret agents became suspicious of us. They secretly sent people to investigate our meetings and later sent the military police to arrest me. They interrogated me twice a day for three hours each time.

The Japanese tortured me for almost a month. One day a Japanese man with a translator came to interrogate me, asking, "Why do you call your meetings 'revival meetings'? Why do you use the term *revival?*" They hated the word *revival,* which can also be translated as *restoration,* because they thought that it implied the restoration of the Chinese nation. The Japanese man who interrogated me was one of the people who had come to investigate our meetings. When he had first come to our meetings, I had given him a small Bible, and that Bible was on the desk beside him. The Lord gave me wisdom, and I did not reply to him right away. It was only after I was sure of his intention that I told him, "All of our practices in the church are according to the Bible. Whatever the Bible has, we also have. Whatever the Bible does not have, we do not have either." Then he asked, "Is the word *revival* in the Bible?" I replied, "Yes, the word *revival* is in the Bible." Then he gave me the small Bible and asked me, "Where is it? Show it to me."

Here is my point—if I had told him that I could not remember where it was and that I would have to spend time to look it up, the consequences would have been unimaginable. However, at that time I remembered that the word *revival* is in Habakkuk, one of the twelve minor prophets. Although I partially remembered the verse, I knew that it would not be easy to find. That day, however, I truly had the Lord's grace. I picked up the Bible and opened it. When I looked down, the page that I was on was Habakkuk 3, and when I placed my finger on that page, my finger pointed to the exact verse that contains the word *revival*—"O Jehovah, revive Your work / In the midst of the years" (v. 2). The Japanese officer was immediately subdued. There are sixty-six books in the Bible, comprising more than a thousand pages, but I was able to turn to the right page and point to the right verse. Thus, he knew that I was not a false preacher.

Hence, you must spend time to study the truth. I hope

you would be familiar with the Bible to such an extent that you would be able to turn to the page and point to the verse that answers the questions that people ask you. This will surely subdue them.

OUR CHARACTER NEEDING TO BE BROKEN THAT WE MAY PARTICIPATE IN THE BUILDING

In the experience of life, the Lord transforms us after we are saved and after He sanctifies us. Based on my own experience, the most difficult part of the Lord's transformation work is the transformation of our character. It is easy to correct a mistake, but it is very difficult to change our character. The Chinese have a saying which says, "Mountains and rivers can be easily changed, but a person's nature is difficult to change." Although we have been regenerated, we may not have had that much transformation, and even if we have had some amount of transformation, not much is seen in our character. I hope you are clear about this point so that you would exercise to be properly transformed in your character.

About fifty years ago, there was a Christian group in Honor Oak, England under the leadership of T. Austin-Sparks. The members of that group were the most spiritual Christians in the world. They never invited outsiders to speak to them. The only exception they made was that they frequently invited Brother Watchman Nee to speak while he was there from 1938 to 1939. In 1956 and 1957 we invited Brother Austin-Sparks twice to minister to us and provided him and his wife with very warm hospitality. When I visited them in 1958, Brother Austin-Sparks returned the courtesy and also gave me hospitality in a very warm way. He invited me to speak on the Lord's Day and held special meetings for me. During my month-long stay there, I clearly saw two things. First, I saw that the British character of those Christians was intact and unchangeable, and second, I saw that they had absolutely no building. Hence, I was clear within that our natural character is not suitable for the building. For the building up of the church, your character, as well as mine, must be broken.

To build a meeting hall, for example, we need bricks, wood,

stone, and steel. To build all these materials together requires that we break them. Suppose a piece of wood or a brick wanted to keep its original appearance and refused to have its long parts cut off, its wide parts sawn off, or its sharp edges sanded down. Consequently, it would have no way to participate in the building. A meeting hall can be built only because every single piece of material has been broken and not one piece remains intact. Similarly, if our character is too strong, and we are not willing to be broken, then it will be impossible for us to participate in the building.

Although the Lord's life is powerful, it encounters an obstacle in us—our character. Our character is more solid than cement. No matter how hard our character is smashed, it cannot be broken, and no matter how much one drills it, it cannot be drilled through. Our character is not only composed of our nature but also of our personality. Nature is inborn, but personality is cultivated. Our character is thirty percent nature and seventy percent habit. For example, suppose a Chinese person is brought to America shortly after his birth. After growing up, he may be Chinese in nature, but he will have an American personality. This indicates that character is composed less of one's nature and more of one's habits. This also shows us the reason why Japanese and Chinese people, even though they have a blood relationship, are different in their character. They are different in character because they are raised in different environments.

The cultivation of a person's character is almost complete by the time he reaches the age of fifteen. Brother Nee once said that if a person's character is not changed before he is fifty years old, then it will be impossible to change his character, because after a person turns fifty years old, his character becomes set and cannot be changed anymore. Throughout my more than sixty years of observation, I have not seen many people under the age of fifty who were willing to be changed through the breaking of their character. I confess that this is not an easy matter. However, I can also testify that this depends on how much you are willing to receive the Lord's grace and whether you are willing to cooperate with the Lord. This altogether depends on your willingness.

NEEDING TO EXERCISE OUR WILL
TO COOPERATE WITH THE LORD
THAT OUR CHARACTER MAY BE CHANGED

Our cooperation with the Lord involves a basic principle in the Scriptures, which is that God created man with a free will, allowing man to have the freedom of choice. Our will can determine our course. Many Jews, for example, have determined not to choose God but to choose money, and in the end they have succeeded. God gave this power of determination to our will when He created man, and God does not interfere with this. In the beginning in the garden of Eden, God put man in front of the tree of life and the tree of the knowledge of good and evil for him to choose. In the same way, God has put us fallen ones in front of our character and Christ's salvation so that we may make a choice. In a sense, today the tree of the knowledge of good and evil is our character, and the tree of life is Christ. Our choice depends on whether we want Christ or our character.

There is only one tree of knowledge of good and evil, yet it has many different expressions, and it always causes you to choose between itself and Christ. Although I do not think that you are absolutely victorious, I believe that the majority of you have overcome the world and sin and have chosen the tree of life. I believe that you would no longer wander in the world or be defiled by sins. Of course, you may still fall, which is why I pray unceasingly with fear and trembling that you would not enter into temptation. However, you are clear that God is versus the world (James 4:4). Outwardly speaking, you also know that God is versus sin (Rom. 3:23). Regarding service, you are clear that God is versus mammon (Matt. 6:24). Therefore, you love God, you do not love the world, you forsake sin, and you do not dream about being rich. These are all expressions of how you have chosen the tree of life and forsaken the tree of the knowledge of good and evil. Now the tree of the knowledge of good and evil that you must forsake is your character. Now that you have joined the Full-Time Training, you must overcome this expression of the tree of the knowledge of good and evil—your character.

OUR GREATEST ENEMY BEING OUR CHARACTER

The Bible says that the last enemy of God is death (1 Cor. 15:26). According to my observation, however, character is the last enemy for those of us who love and pursue the Lord. Twenty years ago a good foundation was laid for our work in the Far East, especially in Taiwan. Yet in the twenty years since then, although by the Lord's mercy our work has not declined, there has not been much development. What is the reason for the lack of development? The reason is not the world, sin, or the influence of material wealth. It is our troublesome character. Our Chinese character is too loose and passive. Without outward pressure in the environment, we become self-content at a certain stage and thus delay the Lord's work.

According to the Chinese character, everything is "fine" and "about the same," as long as we have a bed to sleep in, food to eat, and a house to live in. In the past, prior to the celebration of the Chinese New Year, the northern Chinese would thoroughly clean their homes, but in the days after New Year's Day, their homes would seem "about the same" to them, whether they were clean or dirty. They would not clean their homes again until their homes were so dusty that whatever they touched was covered with dust. Finally, only when they could no longer bear looking at it would they began to wipe off the dust. However, when they would wipe off the dust, they would not do a thorough job, wiping only the center of the room and leaving the four corners dirty. In the matter of cleaning, we can see the Chinese character, which regards everything as being "about the same."

THE GREATEST HINDRANCE TO THE LORD'S WORK IN HIS RECOVERY BEING OUR CHARACTER

Our work in the Far East in the last twenty years has suffered from this character of everything being "about the same." The Lord Jesus rebuked the church in Laodicea for having such an attitude, saying, "You are neither cold nor hot; I wish that you were cold or hot" (Rev. 3:15). If we are cold or hot, the Lord has a way. When we are neither cold nor hot, the Lord has no way. More than twenty years ago, we had the

highest rate of increase of any country in eastern Asia. Even
the opposers could not deny that we had the best gospel work
on the island of Taiwan. However, today others have over-
taken us. What is the reason? After analyzing our history in
the past twenty years, we must confess that our character has
been too loose.

In the 1950s many brothers and sisters were raised up by
the Lord. They truly loved the Lord. They forsook position,
fame, and the wealth of the world and loved the Lord fer-
vently. In 1953, after a few months of training, they went out
and advanced the Lord's work in a relentless way. They were
successful in whatever they did, and wherever they went,
churches were quickly raised up. Within ten years they
had opened up a wonderful situation for the Lord's work.
However, today we find it difficult merely to maintain what
was established. Of course there is an outward reason for
this—when Brother Austin-Sparks visited us, he created
some problems among us, quenching the fire in the brothers
and sisters. However, from that time on the brothers and sisters never got hot again but merely maintained the status
quo. The main, intrinsic, and basic reason for this is that our
character is very poor.

There are some things on the earth that we cannot fully
change but that we can still improve. For example, we cannot
change the earth that was created by God. However, we can
make improvements to our life on earth by improving the
means of transportation and shortening the time required to
travel. Regrettably, although transportation today has been
much improved, our way of working is old and is according to
the old customs. In a sense we have fallen back into our old
ways. This is where the crux of the matter lies. Therefore, we
must seek progress and improvement in every matter, especially in our character. The Chinese mind is very useful, but
the Chinese character ruins things. When our mind does not
match our character, the result is that we do things in a slothful way and are neither earnest nor serious about what we
are doing. The senior co-workers truly love the Lord and have
overcome the tree of the knowledge of good and evil in regard
to the world and sin. However, they are too loose in the matter

of character, and thus, it is often necessary for me to strongly motivate them. Because of the Chinese character, our work in the Far East has greatly suffered.

The saints are advancing in the truth and are pursuing life, but why are they not being perfected in the matter of character? I do not mind taking the trouble to exhort you again and again to pay attention to your character because I know that you will serve the Lord and give yourself to the Lord. After doing so, you may be used by the Lord for twenty years. However, if the "moth" of your bad character continues to stay with you, I am afraid that at a certain time you will be eaten, and your usefulness will be ruined. This would be a terrible thing. Therefore, at the beginning of this training, I will deal with this matter of character again and again. Although you must still pursue and make progress in the four matters of truth, life, the gospel, and service, you must be more serious in the training of your character so that you may be fully equipped. I hope that you would all exercise your will and determine to cooperate with the Lord to deal with your character so that you may become useful vessels in the Lord's hand.

CHAPTER SEVEN

THE INWARD AND OUTWARD FILLING OF THE SPIRIT

We who serve the Lord have two weapons. One is outward and the other is inward. Our outward weapon is the Holy Bible, the Lord's word, which is in our hands. Our inward weapon is the Holy Spirit, who is in our spirit. This is why Paul told us to "receive...the sword of the Spirit, which...is the word of God" (Eph. 6:17), and reminded us, "And do not be drunk with wine, in which is dissoluteness, but be filled in spirit" (5:18). In order to serve the Lord, we must be equipped with the truth in the Scriptures and must also pursue the filling of the Spirit.

THE PRECIOUSNESS OF THE BIBLE

In the past year many of you have spent much time in the Word. I believe that you all are clear that there are two aspects of the filling of the Spirit. One aspect is the filling of the Holy Spirit in life, essentially. The other aspect is the filling of the Holy Spirit in power, economically. You must study further, however, to see which verses in the Bible speak of the essential filling of the Spirit and which verses speak of the economical filling of the Spirit. Then when you go out to teach people, you will be able to quote the Scriptures and speak in a logical way so that people will understand and be convinced.

Five major religions have evolved over the past six thousand years of human history. Of these five major religions, the best religious writing is the Christian Bible. This is a well-known fact. This Bible is far superior to all the famous literary writings of both the past and the present. The Bible is the most precious heritage of mankind. Hence, people often show great respect to those who study the Bible. Even many atheists dare not despise the Bible, acknowledging that the Bible is the most difficult book to deal with. Regardless of how much people have sought to discredit the Bible, the Bible still has not been eliminated from human society. Indeed, this book is the Book of books. Although most people are aware of the existence of such a precious Scripture, they are still quite baffled by the truths contained within it. Therefore, when you go out to preach the truths in the Bible, once people see that you have a Bible in your hand, they will respect you, and when you begin to expound the truth to them, they will gladly receive it.

Although so many philosophies, theories, and "sacred" writings have been written and preserved throughout human history, none of these writings claims that its author is the Lord. Moreover, those who believe in these philosophies and theories do not say that their belief is in the Lord. When people believe in Jesus, however, they say that they have believed in the Lord. This is wonderful. It is also wonderful that the Bible is the only book described as being holy. The Bible is called the Holy Bible. Why is it that the Bible is the only book with such a title? It is because the Bible is in fact the only holy book. We cannot call the earth heaven, because only heaven is heaven. We cannot call iron gold, because only gold is gold, and although copper looks very much like gold, we cannot say that copper is gold. If we refer to a deer as a horse, we create confusion. We cannot do this, because a fact is a fact.

God created all things according to their kind. Even though monkeys resemble humans, we still cannot call a monkey a human. Furthermore, we cannot say that humans evolved from monkeys. Some Europeans are very hairy, yet none of them would ever say that they are European monkeys. Instead, they would call themselves Europeans. In the same way, throughout the six thousand years of human history, thousands and thousands of books have been written and preserved, but only one book is called holy. As such, people cannot help but respect this book. Since people respect the Bible, we must know this book. When we go out to visit people one on one, if we bring the Bible with us and speak to them in a proper way, they will surely respect us.

THE SPIRIT'S INWARD FILLING
BEING MORE PRECIOUS THAN HIS OUTWARD FILLING

Today many Christians pursue the filling of the Spirit. If we meet someone who asks concerning the matter of being filled with the Spirit, we must immediately tell him that according to the Bible there are two aspects of being filled with the Spirit—the outward, economical aspect and the inward, essential aspect. Then we have to exercise our spirit to speak to him with our whole being according to the Bible concerning these two aspects of the Spirit's filling.

The economical aspect of the filling of the Spirit is frequently mentioned in Acts. The first time that it is mentioned is in 2:4. The second time is in 4:8. These verses are the fulfillment of the Lord's promise in 1:8. The essential aspect of the filling of the Spirit is mentioned only once in the entire book of Acts. It is mentioned in 13:52, which says, "The disciples were filled with joy and with the Holy Spirit." The Greek word for *filled* in this verse is *pleroo,* a word which denotes inward filling. This is the aspect of the inward filling of the Spirit essentially. This aspect of the Spirit's filling is for life, not for power. The fact that joy is a matter of life and not of power proves this point. Here the Greek word that is translated *filled* is a different word from the Greek word that is translated *filled* in 2:4 and 4:8.

While I was serving as the editor of *The Christian,* I wrote an article on the filling of the Holy Spirit titled "The Work of the Holy Spirit in the Believers." In 1932 I started to study the New Testament by using Greek-English interlinear reference books. In 1936, while I was editing *The Christian,* I found out that when Luke wrote the book of Acts, he used the word *pletho* in 2:4 and 4:8 and *pleroo* in 13:52. These two words are both translated into English using one word, the word *filled.* Thus, in English there is no apparent distinction. These two Greek words are both derived from the same root, yet they are two different words. In English both words are translated *filled* because there is no other English word that can be used. Nevertheless, we have to see that *pleroo* refers to the inward filling of the Spirit and *pletho* refers to the outward filling of the Spirit.

Acts 6:3a says, "But brothers, look for seven well-attested men from among you, full of the Spirit and of wisdom." Verse 5 continues, "And they chose Stephen, a man full of faith and of the Holy Spirit." The Greek word in these two verses is *pleres*. According to Luke's usage of this word, *pleres* is an adjective form of *pleroo*. When a person is filled with the Spirit essentially (*pleroo*), he is full of the Holy Spirit (*pleres*). I discussed these matters in detail in *The Christian*.

In Acts the word *pleroo* is used in 13:52 with regard to people. In 2:2 it is used with regard to a house—"And suddenly there was a sound out of heaven, as of a rushing violent wind, and it filled the whole house where they were sitting." In 2:2-4 both *pletho* and *pleroo* are used. *Pleroo* is used to describe the wind's filling of the house inwardly, and *pletho* is used to describe the Spirit's filling of people outwardly. This clearly shows us Luke's understanding of these two words. Although Luke's meaning is made clear by studying the Greek words, since both words are translated *filled* in English, it is impossible to tell the difference and know the proper meaning simply by reading the English translation.

To repeat this point again—the word translated *filled* in these verses is two different words in Greek. The word *pleroo* used in 2:2 denotes the filling of a house inwardly; the word *pletho* used in 2:4 denotes the filling of the disciples outwardly. When describing the condition of a person who has been filled inwardly with the Spirit, Luke uses the word *pleres*. Hence, when you speak the truth concerning the filling of the Spirit, first you have to tell people that there are two aspects of the Spirit's filling. One aspect is the outward filling of the Spirit. This aspect is of power and is economical. The other aspect is the inward filling of the Spirit. This aspect is of life and is essential. Regarding the economical aspect of the filling of the Spirit, you can use 2:4, 4:8, and 4:31. Regarding the essential aspect of the filling of the Spirit, you can use 13:52.

Which part of our being does the Spirit fill when He fills us inwardly? According to Ephesians 5:18, He fills us in our spirit. Thus, when we speak of the inward filling of the Spirit, our presentation should be based on Acts 13:52 and Ephesians 5:18. If we speak concerning the outward filling of the Spirit, we need to use the Greek words to prove what we are saying. Hence, I encourage you to always have an interlinear Greek-English New Testament with you so that you can use it at any time to show people the Greek words. If you do this, many of the young people who hear your speaking will believe and be saved.

When we preach the gospel to elderly people, we do not need to reason with them that much, but when we preach the gospel to young people, we need to reason with them a great deal. After you speak to them about the filling of the Spirit, you need to tell them in which part of our being the Spirit fills us. According to the Scriptures, man was created with three parts—spirit, soul, and body (1 Thes. 5:23). Both the spirit and the body are substantial, but the soul is abstract. This is because when God created man, He used only two kinds of material—the dust of the ground and His own breath, which He breathed into man (Gen. 2:7). Dust became man's human body, and the breath became the human spirit. When the two mixed together, this produced man's soul. Therefore, man's soul was not created with a specific material. The human body was created with dust, so our body has all the elements of dust and needs to be maintained by minerals. The human spirit was created with God's breath. This breath, the breath of life, became our spirit.

The human spirit is more important than the human body. This is why Ephesians 5:18 says, "Do not be drunk with wine, in which is dissoluteness, but be filled in spirit." To be drunk with wine is to be filled in the body. Here it says that we should not be filled with wine in our body but that we should be filled in spirit. We need to be filled with Christ unto all the fullness of God (1:23; 3:19). Today all the riches of Christ are included in the life-giving Spirit (1 Cor. 15:45b; 2 Cor. 3:17). To be filled in our spirit is to be filled with the essential Spirit. The essential Spirit is the life-giving Spirit, and the life-giving Spirit is the Spirit of reality as the realization of Christ, referred to in John 14:17.

The essential Spirit had to pass through a process before He could fill us. The essential Spirit is the ultimate consummation of the Triune God. Christ is the embodiment of the Triune God, and the life-giving Spirit is the ultimate consummation of the Triune God (Col. 2:9; 1 Cor. 15:45b). When the ultimate consummation, the ultimate expression, of the Triune God reaches us, He comes to us as the life-giving Spirit, the essential Spirit. We need to be filled with the essential Spirit in our spirit. Ephesians 3:17 says that Christ wants to make His home in our hearts. When we are completely filled with the essential Spirit in our spirit, then Christ as the embodiment of the Triune God will occupy our heart and make His home in our heart. When we are filled in our spirit experientially with the essential Spirit, the ultimate consummation of the Triune God, and when Christ as the embodiment of the Triune God fully occupies, possesses, and makes His home in our hearts, the result will be that we are filled with and occupied by the Triune God completely. This is the significance of the filling of the Spirit.

The inward filling of the Spirit is different from the outward filling of the Spirit. The outward filling of the Spirit is far less precious than the inward filling of the Spirit. Hence, after the book of Acts the word for outward filling is not used in the twenty-two Epistles from Romans to Revelation. Instead, inward filling is emphasized. Although the New Testament uses two different words for the filling of the Spirit and emphasizes the inward filling of the Spirit, the Pentecostal movement regards the two as one thing, thinking that spiritual baptism and drinking of the spiritual drink are the same. This is an incorrect understanding. Among Christians in general, groups such as the Southern Baptist Church and InterVarsity Christian Fellowship almost do not talk about the Spirit at all. Although the Bible mentions the Spirit and they have read about the Spirit, they almost completely ignore the Spirit. Those in the Pentecostal movement, especially those who emphasize tongue-speaking, pay attention to the Spirit, but in doing so, they mix the inward, essential aspect of the Spirit's filling with the outward, economical aspect. As a result, they equate so-called spiritual baptism with drinking of the spiritual drink. This does not correspond to 1 Corinthians 12:13, which says, "For also in one Spirit we were all baptized into one Body...and were all given to drink one Spirit." Here the conjunction *and* indicates that to be baptized and to drink are two matters. To be baptized is to be filled outwardly, and to drink is to be filled inwardly. Therefore, the Pentecostals are mistaken in neglecting the distinction between the two.

I stayed in Shanghai after the second World War. From time to time I ministered in Nanking. At that time there was a saying in the region around the lower Yangtze River. The saying was, "In the morning the skin encompasses the water; at night the water encompasses the skin." When a person drinks tea in the tea house in the morning, his skin "encompasses" the water. When he goes to take a bath at night, the water encompasses the skin. They believed that if one practiced this, he would surely be healthy. After I heard this saying, I found it to be very good and meaningful. The skin encompassing the water is a picture of the inward filling, and the water encompassing the skin is a picture of the outward filling. If you want to be a healthy Christian, you have to be revived every morning. This is the skin encompassing the water. You also need to receive the outward filling of the Spirit when you go out to labor for the Lord at night. This is the water encompassing the skin. The Pentecostals make these two "encompassings" into one "encompassing." As a result, many of them get too deeply immersed in water and drown.

ALLOWING THE HOLY SPIRIT
TO FILL EVERY ROOM OF OUR BEING
THROUGH THOROUGH PRAYER AND CONFESSION

How can we be filled with the Triune God? We can be filled with the Triune God through thorough prayer and confession. When you began the Full-Time Training, you renewed your consecration. This is good, but you also have to find some time in your busy schedule to kneel down before the Lord by yourself and to thoroughly pray and confess. This is most precious. At the beginning of this time, you may tell the Lord, "O Lord, forgive me. Although You have forgiven me of all my sins, I have never had a thorough confession and a thorough dealing. Today I would like to confess all of my sins thoroughly before You. Please shine on me!"

When you pray in this way, do not seek for feeling. You have to believe that the Lord's Spirit is with you. You also do not need to confess according to a sequence. Simply confess according to what you sense within and according to what you remember. Confess your sins to the Lord one by one until, according to your inner sense and your memory, you have nothing more to confess. Once you have done this, you should simply believe that you have been filled in your spirit with the ultimate consummation of the Triune God. Every Christian should have one time in which he thoroughly confesses in this way. In medical science this is equivalent to changing the blood cells in your entire body in order to cleanse away all the germs and filthiness from your system for the sake of your health. Every one of you needs to be filled with the Spirit in this way.

How much the Spirit can fill you within depends on how much room you give Him. The more room you give Him, the more He fills you. Similarly, the amount of air that fills a bottle depends on how much space there is in the bottle. If half of the bottle is filled with soil, air can fill only half of the bottle. The more the soil is removed from the bottle, however, the more the air will fill it. In the same way, the more you remove the defilement of sin and the filthiness that is within you, the more the Holy Spirit will be able to fill you. As you empty out, the Spirit will fill you. When you have completely emptied yourself of all filthiness, then you will also be completely filled with the Spirit.

NEEDING TO PASS THROUGH THE CRISIS
OF BEING FILLED WITH THE SPIRIT

When you have a time with the Lord to confess, do not seek any feeling; just confess and pray thoroughly. To confess is to empty yourself out, and to pray is to receive the Lord into you. Hence, confession plus prayer is a breathing out and a breathing in. We breathe out our sins and breathe in God Himself. A. B. Simpson wrote a hymn that says, "I am breathing out my sorrow, / Breathing out my sin; / I am breathing, breathing, breathing, / All Thy fulness in" (Hymns, #255). Through continuous confession we breathe out our filthiness until all of our uncleanness is gone, and as we breathe out, we also breathe in. As we breathe out our sins, we breathe in God Himself. Thank and praise the Lord that although we are still filthy, He comes to us with His blood as the Lamb-God, the redeeming God. As soon as I breathe out, my sins are gone, and as soon as I breathe in, God comes in. This does not take any effort. As long as I breathe out a little of my sins, I immediately breathe in a little of God. When I confess my sins a little, God comes in to fill me a little. When I have completely breathed out all of my sins, I will be completely filled with God within, completely filled inwardly with the life-giving Spirit as the consummation of the Triune God.

I am not boasting of my seniority, but I have studied this matter for more than fifty years. In the message titled, "The Work of the Holy Spirit in the Believers," I pointed out that the work of the Holy Spirit is first to regenerate us and then to fill us. When I went to the United States, I saw that the Pentecostal movement was very prevailing there. Although the Pentecostals were very prevailing, when I stood up and trumpeted this word concerning the filling of the Spirit, no one was able to say anything to refute me. The truth is with the Lord's recovery. When we put forth the truth of the Bible, no one can refute it.

Both our actual experience and the truth of the Bible give us a clear picture of the inward filling of the Spirit. Those in the Pentecostal movement also talk about confession, but they wrongly teach people that confession must be accompanied by speaking in tongues. The Bible never says that we must speak in tongues to be filled with the Spirit. Today people are hungry and thirsty for God. Thus, those in the Pentecostal movement use tongue-speaking to attract them. Because the Pentecostals lack the truth, they encourage people to pursue after tongue-speaking. Actually, in many cases their so-called speaking in tongues is not genuine. They simply ask people to roll their tongue and speak out anything that comes to their mind. As a result of this practice, they are not filled with the Holy Spirit. They are not even filled with the evil spirits. They are filled only with themselves.

Those in the Pentecostal movement uplift speaking in tongues and encourage those who are hungry and thirsty for God to make speaking in tongues their goal. Actually, their kind of tongue-speaking is often a fraud. I have collected many materials in order to study the matter of tongue-speaking. These materials prove that an ancient form of tongue-speaking has existed in China, Egypt, and Japan. The tongue-speaking practiced by the Corinthians was also prevalent in the Gentile region of Asia Minor. Later this practice spread to the Greek peninsula. A brother from Ghana, Africa told me that when he was around ten years old, he saw a priest of the native religion of his own country also speak in tongues. Therefore, those who have discernment know that the tongue-speaking practiced among the Pentecostals is often not genuine and not according to the truth.

On the one hand, this fellowship is meant to help you by giving you the proper way to pursue the filling of the Spirit. On the other hand, it is meant to give you an inoculation. When you speak to people concerning the filling of the Spirit, they may say, "We also talk about the filling of the Spirit" and may ask you, "Do you speak in tongues?" If you do not know how to answer them, you will be poisoned by them. You must be clear that the filling of the Spirit has two aspects—an outward aspect and an inward aspect. The outward aspect is mentioned only in Acts, but in the Epistles from Romans to Revelation, the inward filling is emphasized because it is the more important aspect.

When we are filled inwardly, what are we filled with? We are filled with the Spirit of life, the essential Spirit, the life-giving Spirit, the Triune God who has been processed and consummated through death and resurrection. When we were saved, the Spirit entered into us. However, there are still many things within us that are not of Him, things that have not been dealt with and are filthy and sinful. Hence, if we want to be filled with the Spirit, we need to go before the Lord to repent, confess, and pray. Through repenting, confessing, and praying, we will breathe out our sins and breathe in God Himself as the life-giving Spirit. Through this breathing out and breathing in, we will be filled with the Spirit.

NEEDING TO BE OBEDIENT AFTER BEING FILLED

Acts 5:32b says, "The Holy Spirit, whom God has given to those who obey Him." This verse reveals that when we breathe in God and are filled with God as the life-giving Spirit, we need to closely follow and obey the Spirit. Obedience is both the way and the requirement for us to receive and enjoy the Spirit of God. Today we must pass through the crisis of being filled with the Spirit. This filling is the inward filling (*pleroo*), but it is also accompanied by the outward filling (*pletho*), because once you are filled inwardly, you will overflow outwardly. If we practice "encompassing the water with the skin" every morning—being filled inwardly in our morning revival, in our prayer, and in our walking according to the Spirit—then we will spontaneously experience the "water encompassing the skin"—the outward filling of the Spirit in our living and work. This is the normal Christian life.

Chapter Eight

FULFILLING THE LAW OF PROPAGATION AND CARING FOR THE PRINCIPLE OF LIFE

THE INWARD AND OUTWARD FILLING OF THE HOLY SPIRIT

We are foolish if we study the truths in the Bible without using the life-study messages and the New Testament Recovery Version. If we want to study the inward and outward filling of the Holy Spirit, it is even more necessary for us to use the life-study messages and the footnotes in the New Testament Recovery Version.

Acts 2:4a says, "And they were all filled with the Holy Spirit." Note 2 of this verse clearly indicates that the word *filled* in Greek is *pletho*. *Pletho*, which is also used in 4:8, 31, 9:17, 13:9, and Luke 1:15, 41, and 67, refers to being filled outwardly. According to its usage in Acts, the Greek word *pleroo* indicates the filling of a vessel within. This word is used in 2:2 to describe the wind's filling of the house. *Pletho* indicates the filling of persons outwardly. This word is used in verse 4 to describe how the Spirit filled the disciples outwardly. The disciples were filled inwardly and essentially *(pleroo)* with the Spirit for their Christian living (13:52); the disciples were filled outwardly and economically *(pletho)* with the Spirit for their Christian ministry. The essential Spirit filled the disciples inwardly by coming into them (John 14:17; Rom. 8:11); the economical Spirit filled the disciples outwardly by coming upon them (Acts 1:8; 2:17). Every believer in Christ should experience both aspects of the filling of the Holy Spirit. Even Christ as a man experienced both aspects. He was born of the Spirit essentially for His being and living (Luke 1:35; Matt. 1:18, 20), and He was anointed with the Spirit economically for His ministry and move (Matt. 3:16; Luke 4:18). The essential Spirit was within Him, and the economical Spirit was upon Him.

Acts 13:52 says, "And the disciples were filled with joy and with the Holy Spirit." Note 1 of this verse shows us that the Greek word *pleroo*, which is translated *filled*, refers to being filled inwardly. This infilling by the Holy Spirit is essential, meaning that it is for life rather than for power. The fact that this verse links being filled with the Holy Spirit to being filled with joy, which is a matter of life, proves this.

Acts 6:3 says, "But brothers, look for seven well-attested men from among you, full of the Spirit and of wisdom." Note 1 points out that the Greek word translated *full* is *pleres*. The way that this word is used in this verse and in 6:5, 7:55, 11:24, and Luke 4:1 shows that it is the adjective form of *pleroo*. Being full of the Spirit is the condition of one who has been filled with the Spirit inwardly and essentially, as mentioned in 13:52. This filling is a matter of life not work.

If we study the notes for the above verses in the New Testament Recovery Version, we will clearly see the distinction between the Greek words *pleroo*, *pletho*, and *pleres*, and we will understand the difference between the inward and the outward filling of the Holy Spirit. I cannot stir up all the saints to study the truth in depth, but I urge all of you full-time trainees to do this. If you do not study the truth in such a way, your function in serving the Lord will be greatly reduced. I would even encourage those of you who are elders to serve the Lord full time. By serving the Lord full time, you will have time to study the truth so that when you teach others, you will be able to do so properly. If you do not have the time to learn the truth, how can you teach others?

FIGHTING THE GOOD FIGHT FOR THE TRUTH

Our shortcoming is that we do not study the truth in depth. In fact, this is the weakness of Christianity as a whole. In Christianity the knowledge of the truth is truly poor. Many think that they understand the truth quite well. Actually, they understand only the historical councils and creeds of the early church. During the lawsuit over the book

The Mindbenders, the opposing party questioned me five mornings a week for three weeks. They had prepared to question me concerning one hundred and nineteen items, but eventually they could question me concerning only nine of them. That was truly the best defense of the truth.

One of the questions that the opposers asked me concerned what I said at the end of one of the messages in the *Life-study of Genesis*. In that message I said that the local churches are today's "ark" (pp. 393-398). They thought that they had found my fault and strongly declared that my speaking was completely nonsensical. After their lawyer questioned me, however, he himself agreed that I was able to give a detailed explanation of what I had said in the *Life-study of Genesis*. In answering their question, I spoke about Abel, Enosh, Enoch, and then Noah and said that God has a particular work in each age. I told them that God's work during the age of Abel was for men to receive His redemption and to serve Him according to the way of His redemption. In the age of Enosh God had another work. His work in the age of Enosh was for men who had received His redemption to realize their vanity and emptiness so that they would call on the name of Jehovah to receive His riches. In the age of Enoch, God had a further work. His work in this age was that men would not only call on His name and receive His riches, but that they would also learn to walk with God and never leave Him. When it came to the age of Noah, God had an even further work. His work in the age of Noah was that men would not only walk with Him but that they would also build an ark.

I told them that our God has been progressing from one age to the next and that in principle His special move, His special work, in the present age is to recover the church, that is, to build up the local churches. I explained to them that this is why I used a figure of speech to say that the local churches are today's "ark." I told them that this is why I spoke of the ark as a type of the local churches. My explanation left them speechless and exposed their lack of the knowledge of the truth. Over the course of three weeks, their mistakes were exposed one by one, and they could not fight back. Their last question was whether or not I agreed with the doctrines that *The Mindbenders* identifies as orthodox doctrines. Most Christians know the orthodox Christian doctrines; however, *The Mindbenders* said that only the teachings given by Jesus Christ to the twelve disciples when He was on the earth are orthodox. I told them that this was altogether wrong. If only the teaching given by Christ to His twelve disciples were orthodox teachings, then Paul's fourteen Epistles, which constitute a great part of the twenty-seven books of the New Testament, would not be counted as orthodox because Paul was not one of the twelve disciples and Paul never heard any of the messages spoken by Jesus Christ when He was on the earth. I further explained that this understanding contradicts what the Lord Jesus said in John 16:12-13—"I have yet many things to say to you, but you cannot hear them now. But when He, the Spirit of reality, comes, He will guide you into all the reality; for He will not speak from Himself, but what He hears He will speak; and He will declare to you the things that are coming." In these verses the Lord Jesus clearly says that He did not tell the disciples all of the truths and that when the Spirit came, He would declare more truths to them. When the Spirit came, He surely declared many truths to the apostle Paul. This is why the fourteen Epistles written by the apostle Paul were included in the New Testament and are publicly recognized as orthodox.

The day after they questioned me about this matter, all of the main responsible ones among them examined the questions and answers given during the depositions. Soon after this they accepted the settlement agreement, and we won a complete victory.

THE NECESSITY OF EXERTING EFFORT
TO THOROUGHLY STUDY AND TEACH THE TRUTH

Today's Christian theological seminaries teach theology but do not touch the deep truths of the Bible. They touch only the superficial things related to the Bible, such as the number of books and authors of the Bible, how many years it took for the Bible to be written, and where each book was written. They teach only shallow matters, such as the creeds and decisions made by the councils, biblical history, and biblical geography.

Regardless of whether you have been saved many years or you have only recently been saved, most of you probably do not know that the truths in the Lord's recovery are the cream of all the truths in the Bible. In Christianity you cannot find the expressions *transformation, enjoying the Lord, dispensing,* or *economy.* All of these truths are foreign to most of the believers in Christianity. They are ignorant of these high-peak truths, yet some were so foolish as to attack us. This is the pitiful condition of today's Christianity. The truths among us are truly abundant. This is why you need to exert effort to get into them. You are the most blessed group of people in this age. You have graduated from college, forsaken your future, given up everything to pursue the Lord, and put all your time and energy into the Lord's recovery. For this reason, I will do the best I can to help you.

Brother Nee and I spent more than sixty years to study the truth. He began to pursue the truth in 1920, and in 1922 he began to publish periodicals that expounded the truths of the Bible. He carried out his ministry for thirty years until 1952. In 1952 Brother Nee was imprisoned. He remained in prison for twenty years until he went to be with the Lord in 1972. When I was in mainland China, a few brothers and I were under Brother Nee's leadership. In 1949 Brother Nee sent me to Taiwan, and for the past thirty years since 1950 I have been publishing books in Taiwan. Over the past sixty years in the Lord's recovery we have dug out nearly all the truths in the Bible—Brother Nee in the first thirty years and I in the last thirty years. I dare not say that we have dug thoroughly, but I can say that we have opened up the treasure stores, the mines, of the truths in the Bible and have put them before you. There is still much more for you to dig. If the Lord would give me the time to do so, I would rewrite the notes in the New Testament Recovery Version and conduct a life-study of the entire Bible once more. It is a pity that I do not have the time. Nevertheless, I praise and thank the Lord that Brother Nee and I have opened up the riches of the Bible to you. Now you need to dig deeper. We put our whole being into the study of the Word in order to get into its depths. You must dig into the Bible in the same way.

EXERTING EFFORT IN LEARNING LANGUAGES AND IN WRITING

Understanding the truths of the Bible requires the learning of languages. The original language of the New Testament is Greek, and the original language of the Old Testament is Hebrew. It would be good for you to exert some effort to learn these two languages. Moreover, although you are probably quite proficient in understanding and reading Chinese, your mother tongue, you most likely encounter difficulty when you are trying to express the truth. This shows two things—that you are deficient in the skill of writing and that your knowledge of the truth is still vague. Moreover, in the recovery we often speak the truth in English. Thus, if you have not adequately learned English, your understanding of the truth will not be precise. Therefore, I hope that you would have sufficient knowledge of languages and of writing.

Yesterday I fellowshipped with the saints who serve in the bookroom. I said that in 1952 and 1953 I began to conduct trainings here. These trainings went on for ten years, with at least four months of training per year. Although so many were trained, no one has pursued and made adequate progress with regard to languages and writing. As a result, not one can write something that is weighty. This should serve as a warning to us. Thus, I am here to encourage the younger generation to exert effort to learn languages and to learn to write. When I began to serve the Lord in 1932, I felt that there was a lack in my learning. Therefore, I asked someone to buy me an Interlinear Greek-English New Testament in Shanghai so that I could study Greek by myself. I truly hope that in the Lord's work you would not be average persons. Instead of being average, you should be learned ones. To speak in worldly terms—since you have decided to be in this trade, you need to look like one who is in this trade and be an expert in this trade. Do not follow the condition of Christianity. I do not despise those who are in Christianity, and I have no intention to condemn them, but the Lord's work and His move have been hindered due to their shallowness. The Lord needs us to clear the way so that He can move on. If you would be desperate to learn, the Lord would have a free way among you to carry on His work.

THE REACTION OF TODAY'S ORTHODOX CHRISTIANITY

All of Christianity in America was shaken up due to the lawsuit. This was not an ordinary matter, and there have not been many lawsuits in the history of Christianity. I hope that you all would read the "Statement of Decision" that was issued at the close of the lawsuit over the book *The God-Men*. This statement has to do with the content of our contending for the truth.

The lawsuit also caught the attention of Dr. J. Gordon Melton, the chief editor of *The Encyclopedia of American Religions*. This encyclopedia has a very good standing in Christian society and even in American society in general. Dr. Melton studied our truths and felt that they were fundamental and even worthwhile for Christians to read through. He then voluntarily published a book to testify on our behalf. This was more than we ever expected. I had never seen Dr. Melton's face and I had never exchanged letters with him, yet he still recommended me. He said that I am the most outstanding teacher in the local churches and that my theology is altogether based on the Brethren theology, which is the most orthodox theology. Today Christians all over the world recognize that the Brethren theology is the best theology of all orthodox theology. What Dr. Melton said was absolutely right. We have been much influenced by the Brethren truths since the early times. Their theology is in the marrow of our bones. Hence, when our writings are published, they naturally bear the Brethren flavor.

The more effort you exert to know the truth, the more advantageous it will be to you. Any effort you exert to learn the truth will never be wasted effort. You are all blessed, because the publications in the Lord's recovery are very rich. They include all the fundamental truths of the Bible. Thus, there is no need for you to try to collect riches from the writings of others. I dare not say that our speaking is complete, but I would say that there is surely no lack of truth for you to study in our books. The notes in the New Testament Recovery Version alone can almost serve as a compass for all the truths among us. Concerning the matter of the filling of the Spirit, for example, all you have to do is read the notes for Acts 2:4, 6:3, and 13:52, and you will be clear. To know the meaning of transformation, you just need to look up the notes for 2 Corinthians 3:18. I hope that you would deepen your efforts to learn the truth.

THE KNOWLEDGE AND EXPERIENCE OF LIFE BEING OUR URGENT NEED

In addition to studying the truth, you also need to pursue life, and in pursuing life, you should carefully read two books—*The Knowledge of Life* and *The Experience of Life*. The introduction to *The Knowledge of Life* and the preface to *The Experience of Life* clearly point out that although many saints have pursued life over the past two thousand years, no one has been able to clearly explain the various stages of spiritual life and the points one should know to progress along the path of life. In these two books I present these matters in a scientific way. Many of the points contained in these books cannot be found in any of the books of Christianity. No one has ever spoken concerning the three lives and four laws or regarding the nineteen points of the four stages of the spiritual life. Therefore, you have to endeavor to get into these two books and to pursue, stage by stage, the four stages of the spiritual life.

FULFILLING THE LAW OF PROPAGATION AND CARING FOR THE PRINCIPLES OF LIFE

I am worried that the saints in the churches may think that our current emphasis is on preaching the gospel and on the small groups, that our focus is on propagating and gaining increase, and that we are neglecting the matter of life. This is wrong. I hope that you would all experience life in a solid way and realize that everything in the universe has its laws and principles. Science searches out the laws and principles of the universe. For example, the law of human reproduction is contained in marriage. Without marriage, humans cannot reproduce. Therefore, God created our first ancestors as a couple so that they would be fruitful and multiply (Gen. 1:27-28).

Anyone who abides by the law of propagation will reproduce, but this does not mean that what they produce will be acceptable. Lot and his daughters illustrate this point. They abode by this law and had two children—Moab and Ammon (19:30-38). However, the Moabites and Ammonites were not permitted to enter into the holy congregation of Jehovah for ten generations (Deut. 23:3). This shows us that we cannot care only for the fulfillment of the law of propagation and neglect the principle of life. Lot and his daughters acted according to the law of propagation, but they did so in violation of the law of morality. Their way of propagation did not care for the principles of life and human ethics. This was altogether wrong.

I say this to warn you. You must not focus only on propagation and increase while neglecting the law of life. We have led many people to salvation, but are they people of the holy congregation, or are they Moabites and Ammonites? When you go out to work on the campus and to preach the gospel, you cannot care only for the law of propagation and not care for the proper procedure. In my view our campus work is somewhat leaning toward the way of the world. What is the proper procedure of propagation? The proper procedure is as follows: first, we must endeavor to preach the gospel, and second, we must use the small groups. If you do these two things and you do not take the worldly ways, you will have propagation and increase.

We should not criticize others. We should simply exercise strict control over ourselves. We should not fulfill the law of propagation yet violate the principle of life. It is possible to carry out the law of propagation when seeking increase but violate the law of the spiritual life. If we do this, we will have results similar to that of Lot. We may bear children, but these children will not be able to enter into the holy congregation and will be condemned. In the past many evangelists have saved thousands of people, but in principle many of the ones they brought forth may have been "Moabs" and "Ammons" who were not permitted to enter into the holy congregation of Jehovah. Today we have to carry out the law of propagation that God has ordained, but we also have to care for the principle of the spiritual life. Therefore, we need to be those who are orthodox, and our way should be proper. The proper way is to labor on and build up the small groups. This way is different from the way of Christianity.

Many denominations and Christian groups fulfill the law of propagation, yet they do so by utilizing many human methods. For example, they use social activities to attract people and to bring them in. Some groups even use rock music. To do this is to violate the principle of the spiritual life. Because they violate this principle, few of those who are saved by them are in the holy congregation. Of course, there are also "Ruths" among them who receive the Lord's special mercy to seek after Him and to choose Christ. These ones have turned and have entered the holy congregation. My intention in fellowshipping with you about these matters is not to criticize people. My hope is only that you would understand that even though some denominations and Christian groups bring people to salvation, this does not mean that their principle of life is right or is approved by God.

Thirty years ago our rate of increase was very rapid. In five or six years, we had a one hundredfold increase. There are only a few groups in the whole world that have ever had this rate of increase. This was thirty years ago. Within the last fifteen years, however, many groups have surpassed us in their propagation and level of increase. Nonetheless, just because they are ahead of us does not mean they do not have any problems. When a person is running on a racecourse, he will be disqualified if he violates any of the rules. With propagation and increase, however, there is more involved than merely being disqualified, because there is also the question of the children who are begotten. Lot made a mistake, but if he had not begotten any children, he would only have been "disqualified." However, because he begot Moab and Ammon, he also brought harm to the people of Israel. Today many individuals and groups care only for their goal but not for their means or for the principle of life. We cannot be this way.

Today we need to care both for the goal and for the means. Our goal is propagation, and our means is life. I believe that when we care for our means in carrying out the law of propagation, we will definitely have increase. Thirty years ago we took care of these two aspects, and we produced the proper result. Thirty years later we are still for the law of life—we do not love the world, we do not touch sin, we break bread, and we pray in a devout and timely way. However, in the aspect of the work, we have not been carrying out the law of propagation. We have not labored, and we have not had the small groups. We simply "submitted to the will of the heavens," and "let nature take its course." The result is that our propagation stopped. Therefore, today we not only need to care for the principle of life, but we also need to carry out the law of propagation. We cannot bring forth children by violating the law of life and committing "incest." Begetting children is right and necessary, but we cannot do it by any means that we choose without caring for the principle of life.

It is impossible to hear the truths that we have among us anywhere in Christianity. This is because they do not have this light, and they lack this revelation. This proves that we have received the Lord's mercy and are particularly blessed. Since this is the case, you have to seize the opportunity to be one who is strong and pure for the testimony of the Lord's recovery. The way of the Lord's recovery is far-reaching, and the future of the Lord's recovery is very broad. Even though the principle of life limits us, I believe that by being under it the Lord's recovery will expand and spread to all the continents of the earth. This will prepare a way for the Lord to gain His bride and will give Him a way to come back.

The situation in today's Christianity is that although multitudes of people have been saved, few have entered the holy congregation. How then can the Lord come back? Even though propagation is good and increase is necessary, we still need to ask, "How are children being born? Who gave birth to them? Were they born of Lot and his daughters or of Abraham and Sarah?" You have to consider my words as a serious warning. When we carry out the law of propagation, we must be under the principle of life. For this reason we must have the knowledge of life, and we must also have the genuine experience and growth in life. Then we will avoid Lot's mistake and avoid producing descendants in an improper way.

CHAPTER NINE

CHARACTER TRAINING
FOR THE LORD'S SERVICE

NOT BEING SLOTHFUL IN DILIGENCE
BUT BEING FERVENT IN SPIRIT

Romans 12:11 speaks concerning the Body life. This verse says, "In diligence not slothful; fervent in spirit; serving the Lord" (ASV). In this short verse four matters are mentioned—being diligent, not being slothful, being fervent in spirit, and serving the Lord. Apparently these matters are not involved with our character, but actually they are altogether related to our character.

A slothful person will surely have an improper character. I have never met a person who had a strict character and yet was lazy. If you are a lazy person with a slothful character, you cannot be diligent. It is impossible for a lazy person to be diligent because being diligent requires too much effort. According to a lazy person, the best thing to do is to not do anything and to not care about anything.

A person who is diligent will spontaneously be fervent in spirit. In other words, a fervent spirit follows diligence. If you are a slothful person, you will not be fervent in spirit. Instead, you will be extremely cold in spirit. It is quite difficult to start a fire in a refrigerator, but it is very easy to start a fire where there are gas vapors or gasoline. Hence, starting a fire is not only a matter of the fire itself, but it is also a matter of what is used to start it. If you are fervent in spirit, you will be like gas vapors or gasoline and will be easily kindled by even a little contact.

D. L. Moody was a powerful gospel preacher. He once said that he had never seen a lazy person get saved. This is true. I have been preaching the word for many years, and I also have not seen a lazy person get saved. This shows that a lazy person is one who is loose in character, who does not care about anything, and who is indifferent toward everything. He is lazy to such an extent that he does not even want to get saved. I have seen two kinds of young people. One kind is diligent, and the other kind is slothful. The diligent ones are concerned about everything wherever they are. Even when they are staying in other people's homes, they are concerned about whether or not the doors and windows are locked and the lights are turned off. The slothful ones, however, are so lazy that they would not care even if the house were burning down. In a gospel meeting if there are many gospel friends who are diligent, this is an indication that many will get saved. Regrettably, if there are many in the meeting who are lazy, then you should not expect them to give you a quick response, because they will be too lazy to respond.

Today the most important matter regarding our service to the Lord is that we must be fervent and burning in spirit. Whether or not our spirit can be burning depends very much on our character. We should not expect a loose person to be burning within. It is difficult even to start a fire in such a one. According to my observation, those who are genuinely spiritual tend to have quick dispositions. It is difficult for a slow person to become spiritual. Brother Watchman Nee was greatly helped by Miss M. E. Barber, who was much older than he. I never met her, but many who had met her told me that she was a very quick person. Of course, a person who has a quick disposition and does things in a rush also tends to make many mistakes. A wooden chair or a statue of Mary will never make any mistakes because it never moves. Therefore, it is also worthless to be slow. It is difficult for the Holy Spirit to touch a slow person because such a person is indifferent. Everything you say is about the same to him, making it difficult to touch him.

If you have ever lived in the brothers' and sisters' houses, then you have probably discovered that those with a quick temperament are usually the first ones to be touched when listening to a message in the meeting, while those who are slow are seldom touched. Sometimes when you weep for the slow ones, instead of being touched, they ask why you are weeping. Perhaps you have been moved to such an extent that you are in the third heavens, and your whole being has been set on fire by the inner fire, yet they remain puzzled. The reason they are like this is that they are loose and poor in their character. According to what I know, those who do well in school are those who are strong in character. The first ones to believe in the Lord and the most fervent ones in the pursuit of spirituality are those who are strong in character. It is very easy for the Holy Spirit to work on those who are strong in character. When we preach the gospel to students, what we fear the most is meeting people who are like jellyfish, because people like this are poor in character. They drag their feet and are indecisive about everything.

THE RELATIONSHIP BETWEEN OUR CHARACTER AND OUR SERVICE IN THE COORDINATION IN THE BODY

The subject of Romans 12 is the living and service in the Body of Christ. In the service in the Body, those who are the most difficult to coordinate with are those who are weak in character. Hence, Paul's speaking in verse 11 is focused on character. If a person is poor in character, there is no way for him to coordinate with others because his spirit cannot be set on fire. If you observe those who pursue the Lord together and then check your own experience, you will find that it is not easy for those who are loose in character to be touched in their spirit. They are not touched when they read the Bible, nor are they touched when they listen to a message. When listening to a testimony, they think that there is nothing remarkable about it. To those who have a poor character, everything is about the same. Even when there is a great sense of urgency, they remain unmoved.

In the early years of my experience of preaching the gospel, what I feared the most was meeting people who were lazy. Moreover, whenever I went out to labor, I was very afraid of having co-workers who were loose in their character. In mainland China we were always in a hurry to catch the train.

Because of this, whenever I went out to labor with a co-worker who was loose in character, I always needed an extra supply of the Lord's grace and patience. I had to do everything for these ones, because regardless of how much I tried to hurry them, they would still be very slow and unhurried. Thus, many matters were delayed.

I truly appreciate you young brothers and sisters who are giving up your future and consecrating all that you have to the Lord in your youth. However, what concerns me the most is the matter of your character. The Chinese environment in particular is a major hindrance to the building up of a proper character. For over fifty years I have been fighting the battle in the Lord's recovery, and part of the battle has been related to our character. I admit that I have not gotten through in this matter. A Chinese proverb says that changing one's nature is harder than changing mountains and rivers. This is not an exaggeration. It is truly difficult to change one's character. You are here to be trained so that you may be formed into an army to go to the villages for the spread of the gospel. Whether you succeed or fail in this matter will depend on your character training today.

THE PROBLEM OF CHARACTER

First Timothy 4:12 says, "Let no one despise your youth." Not only are young people often despised because of their youth, but even older people are despised when they act like children. In today's society, those who have successful careers or are given authority over others have a strict character. A person with a loose character cannot be a manager or director. Even if he is very knowledgeable and capable, no one will dare to hire him as a manager or a director. If he were given a job, he would be unable to accomplish anything and would end up causing disaster. Do not think that it is easy to be a manager. If you were asked to be a manager, you probably would not be able to do it for even one day. Your subordinates, as well as your superiors, would push you and put pressure on you. If you have a loose character and are unable to bear pressure, eventually you will become seriously ill or at least have stomach ailments.

The difficulty in the Lord's work is that there are no examinations or grading systems for the co-workers. Today every government organization has general and special examinations for their employees, and private companies also have grading systems to assess a person's individual performance. However, there is nothing of this sort in the Lord's work. The co-workers do not have to take examinations, nor will they ever be dismissed. When Brother Nee was taking the lead among the co-workers in mainland China, he suffered much because of the co-workers. Sometimes he was pressed to the limit and wanted to speak some rebuking words to them, but some of the co-workers could not stand being rebuked. They had no fear, so when they were rebuked, they would get angry. They were like hot potatoes that you want to get rid of but cannot and that hurt you when you keep them in your hands. If those brothers had been working in various professions in the world, they would have been asked to leave and to look for another job. However, we cannot do this in the Lord's work. Thus, we are in a difficult situation.

I hope that this would not cause you to consider yourself fortunate to be in the Lord's work and to say within yourself, "I am going to join this profession, because once I am in, no one will have control over me." It is true that no one will control you, but if you have this kind of intention, you will be finished and will be useless in the Lord's hand. There is a saying in northern China that says, "Once a person becomes a soldier, he is like iron beaten into a nail; once a person becomes a preacher, for his whole life he is spoiled." Once iron is beaten into a nail, it has no other use except as a nail. In the eyes of the world, a person who becomes a preacher will eventually be good for nothing. His whole life will be finished. Thus, our character needs to be under strict control and to be molded all the time. If we are careless and become set in a certain mold, we will be finished. However, who will control us while we are doing the Lord's work? Even though Timothy was a spiritual son to Paul, the most Paul could do was to write to him in the way of an exhortation. If Timothy received the exhortation, Paul would be comforted, but if he rejected the exhortation, Paul would not be able to do anything. History proves that Paul was able to get through with Timothy and was unable to get through with other co-workers (2 Tim. 4:10). Even his letters to them were of no effect.

Our hope is to produce two hundred young, full-time serving ones in Taiwan each year. If the Lord fulfills this matter, we will have one thousand full-time serving ones in five years. Although this sounds encouraging, I am concerned that when you young people enter into the Lord's work, you will become one thousand "hot potatoes" if your character is not trained properly. If this happens, then we will not be able to do the Lord's work. Hence, I emphasize again and again that besides pursuing the truth and growing in life you must also cultivate a strict character. If you do not pursue the truth or grow in life that much, it is not too great a problem. You may not have a great measure of usefulness, but at least you will still be able to exercise your portion. However, if you learn the truth and grow very well in life but are not built up in character, then this will become a great problem.

The senior co-workers among us are getting old, and in a sense, they cannot do that much anymore. There are some other co-workers, but I would not like to talk about them right now. Thus, I have a heavy burden concerning you young people. I hope that you would pay full attention to the matter of your character. Formerly in China there was a group of people who were known as Bohemians. They did not button their shirts, tie their shoes, or comb their hair. The only thing that they ever did was to stretch out their hand when tea was brought and open their mouth when food was served. Those people were lazy. You should not imitate them. Rather, you should learn to be diligent. A young brother once testified that when he was in the military, he was very disciplined and orderly. He arranged all his personal belongings in a tidy manner, and even his superior praised him. Later, however, after he retired from the military and got married, he needed his wife to help him find his watch, socks, and clothes. This shows that a good character had not been built up in him. Recently, after hearing about the importance of character, he was awakened. He realized that this is a great matter, so he made up his mind to be trained in character and asked his wife not to help him find his daily necessities. If you sisters are serving the Lord and marry this kind of husband, do not help him to do anything. Rather, help him to be trained in his character.

In the churches most problems, whether big or small, can be easily solved. The most difficult matter is finding a proper elder to manage the affairs of the church. The reason it is difficult to find such an elder lies in the matter of character. Therefore, do not despise the training that you are receiving. After you graduate from the training and go out to labor for the Lord, you must in a sense be like a "suicide squad." Those who have not built up their character cannot be like those in a suicide squad. On January 28, 1932, Japan invaded Shanghai. At that time a pilot in the Chinese air force piloted his plane into a Japanese aircraft carrier. This action shook the whole world. The various world powers were fearful of the bravery of the Chinese people and warned Japan not to act rashly and blindly anymore. This temporarily stopped the Japanese invasion. My point in saying this is that your ability to take a certain action altogether hinges on your character. That young pilot was brave and could sacrifice himself to save the country because he was a person of good character. If he had not had a good character, he would not have been able to do such a thing. Today in the Lord's service, those who have a good character and a goal are very much needed.

Whether or not we will fulfill the Lord's purpose has much to do with our character in spiritual matters and in the matters of our daily living. All parents know that if they want their children to be useful, they must cultivate in them a good character. If their character is not built up, they will be easily spoiled. Although you have received a certain amount of perfecting and training regarding your character, in order for you to be useful in the Lord's hand and to serve the Lord, you need further training regarding your character.

A person who is loose in his character cannot be three-dimensional and is like a flat, two-dimensional surface. A two-dimensional person cannot be a vessel and cannot contain anything. If you are not built up in your character, you will be a person who is flat and cannot be useful. Hence, in learning to serve the Lord, the foremost matter is to pay attention to your character. You cannot be loose in this matter. For instance, consider your reading of the Bible. You must decide how much to read and then read according to a schedule. You must read even when you are sick or when you are exceedingly busy. You must carefully evaluate and schedule every aspect of your life and try your best to save your time and energy for your service and spiritual pursuit. Whether or not you will have good fellowship with the Lord, have adequate prayer before the Lord, read the Lord's Word properly, or advance in your usefulness in the Lord's hand will depend on your character. If your character is loose, none of these things can be built up.

SIX ASPECTS RELATED TO CHARACTER IN 2 TIMOTHY 2

In 2 Timothy 2 Paul used six kinds of people to depict a person who serves the Lord. He also referred to some matters related to character in order to train his young co-worker. Verses 3 and 4 say that we who serve the Lord as good soldiers of Christ Jesus should not entangle ourselves with the affairs of this life. This requirement is absolutely related to our character. We cannot fulfill this requirement if our character is lacking. Verse 5 speaks about a person who contends in the games. It likens a person who serves the Lord to an athlete who competes in the Olympic games. In order to win a game, an athlete must receive strict training. Some coaches not only teach their athletes skills but also train their character by controlling their diet, sleep, and dress. If an athlete is loose in his character and does not eat, sleep, live, and walk according to a schedule, he will not be able to win the game.

Verse 6 mentions the laboring farmer. A lazy farmer is destined to fail because a farmer must labor in order to succeed. The word *labor* implies diligence and toil. Thus, this is a matter of character. Verse 15 says, "Be diligent to present yourself approved to God, an unashamed workman, cutting straight the word of the truth." Here the word *workman* refers to a carpenter, and the cutting straight of the word is likened to the work of carpentry. Paul was telling Timothy to unfold the Word of God in its various parts rightly and straightly without distortion, just as a carpenter cuts a piece of wood. When a piece of wood is cut crookedly, it becomes completely useless. If you are not strict enough in your character, your reading of the Word will be loose and your interpretation of the Word will be inaccurate. If you take the attitude that everything is "about the same," then your interpretation of the Word will also be "about the same." Only those who are strict in character can cut straight the word of the truth.

Verse 21 says, "If therefore anyone cleanses himself from these, he will be a vessel unto honor, sanctified, useful to the master, prepared unto every good work." A vessel unto honor has to meet a certain standard that it may contain a specific object of honor. Here the word *honor* is related to our nature, the word *sanctified* indicates our position, the word *useful* implies the matter of function, and the *prepared* reveals the matter of training. Paul exhorted Timothy to cleanse himself from the vessels of dishonor that he could be trained in these four matters. These four items together would make Timothy a vessel unto honor according to a certain standard. This also involves our character.

Verses 24-25 say, "But a slave of the Lord ought not to contend but be gentle toward all, apt to teach, bearing with wrong; in meekness correcting those who oppose." It is wonderful that when Paul spoke about being a slave of the Lord, he did not say that such a one should read the Bible, pray, grow in life, or pursue the truth. Neither did he say that such a one should develop his eloquence, utterance, and gifts. Rather, he said that a slave of the Lord ought not to contend but to be gentle in his attitude. Those who contend are loose in their character. Those who are strict in their character do not contend and have no time to contend. A policeman always carries a gun with him. If he has not been strictly trained, the gun can be very dangerous to him because he might pull it out and shoot carelessly. A tendency to contend is proof that a person does not have the power to restrain or control himself. His power of self-restriction is poor. Because his character is poor, it is easy for him to contend with others. When you go out to labor for the Lord, you may encounter people who will argue. Old people will argue with you, Buddhists will argue with you, and those who have scientific minds will also argue with you. If you can avoid arguing with them and simply give them the truth, then you will be a very skillful worker. This requires much self-control and self-restraint. This kind of character is hard to build up.

This is the training that Paul gave Timothy. By reading these few points, we can see that a person who serves the Lord must be a soldier, an athlete who runs on the racecourse, a farmer who labors in the field, a carpenter who cuts wood, a vessel unto honor, and a slave of the Lord. If you study these six kinds of people carefully, you will realize that they are altogether related to the matter of character. Once the problem of character is solved and your character is built up, you will be a good soldier, a good athlete, a good farmer, a good workman, a good vessel, and a good slave. I hope that you would concentrate all of your effort on this matter of building up your character in your living, your walk, your conduct, your speaking, and your attitude whether at home, abroad, at work, or in the church, so that you may be very useful in the Lord's hand.

Question: In the past you spoke about the thirty character traits that require training. Like you, we feel that this matter is very important. However, we do not know the secret of how to be trained. Moreover, although those who have a poor character are like "hot potatoes," we cannot allow them to remain the same. Are there any secrets to helping such people?

Answer: The answer lies in your determination. You must be determined to consecrate yourself to the Lord to become a useful vessel in His hands. You need to labor with such a determination. The secret of your labor is to exercise not to be loose but strict in all things, whether big or small. The foundation depends on your exercise in your practical daily life. For example, you should be exercised in returning something to the place from which you took it, in paying attention to tidiness and neatness, and in doing things according to a plan. Once you begin to exercise in this way, you will realize how loose you were in the past. If you appreciate and are touched by this kind of fellowship but do not exercise or labor in your daily living, this fellowship will be completely useless to you.

You also have to help one another and be willing to be reminded of this matter at any time. Do not merely try to keep the peace with one another by being polite. Instead, you must go before the Lord, have adequate prayer, and ask the Lord for enlightenment and guidance. I know that these are not easy matters. It is helpful to remind a child who is three or five years old. However, such reminders may not be of much use to those of you who are already set in your ways. This altogether depends on you. If you are not determined and do not exercise, then there will be no way for you to be trained. If you are willing to take this matter seriously and spare no effort to carry it out, then it will be easy for you to be trained. From this perspective, it is better for you to be strict than to be loose. Even to be overly strict is all right, because it may be necessary to be overly strict in order to effectively correct our defects.

I am full of joy to see that you have made a great improvement in your dress. This proves that you are determined and willing to be reminded. I spoke a strong word to the elders that if they want to manage the affairs of the church, the first thing they need to do is to clean the meeting hall and put it in order. Some elders and co-workers keep their homes clean and tidy but have no feeling concerning the dirtiness and untidiness of the meeting hall. They say that they love the Lord, but actually they love themselves. If you truly loved the Lord, you would arrange and decorate the meeting hall, which is being used for the Lord's work, so that it would look nicer than your own home. By the Lord's mercy, I can tell you that when I was laboring for the Lord in Taiwan, I used the best toilets and bathtubs for the meeting halls and workers' homes, but for my own home I used very simple furnishings.

If you want to serve the Lord full time, first you must be trained in your character. Second, you must view the Lord's work as far more important than anything else. You must consider everything that is related to the Lord's work as the most important. This also involves our character. Therefore, I hope that you all would seriously be trained in your character from the very beginning of your training. In this way, all the meeting halls in Taiwan will be changed in appearance, not to be extravagant or to make a vain show but to be elegant, presentable, neat, and tidy, and to meet every need. Whether or not the Lord's work can be successful today depends on the training of your character. I hope you all would receive this word.

Prayer: Lord, Your words were found, and we ate them. Lord, cause us not to reject this word, and enable us to fully receive and amen Your word. We do not want to say, "This word is hard; who can hear it?" Lord, cause us to exercise our spirit to receive it. Your speaking such a word to us proves that You are merciful and gracious to us. We want to say amen to Your word. May Your word transform us. Lord, make us good soldiers, good athletes, good farmers, good workmen, vessels unto honor, and good slaves to You. We pray that You would remember our desire and grant us grace upon grace so that we may seriously practice this in our daily living. Amen!

CHAPTER TEN

THREE MATTERS REQUIRING THE ATTENTION OF THE LORD'S SERVING ONES

THE FUNDAMENTAL MATTERS IN OUR SERVICE TO THE LORD

If we would examine our experiences according to the Bible, we would realize that all of us who serve the Lord need to continually pay attention to three fundamental matters. This does not mean that there are only three matters that we must pay attention to but that these three matters are the most fundamental. The first matter is building up our character, the second matter is being equipped with the truth, and the third matter is being filled with the Holy Spirit.

THE BUILDING UP OF OUR CHARACTER

In 1953 while I was holding a training, I used an illustration to explain the matter of character. Almost all textile products, whether cotton or silk, must be put into dyeing tubs to be dyed. The dye, when used on the coarsest and worst fabric, does not appear beautiful, but when the same dye is used on the best Chinese silk, the outcome is beautiful and shiny. There is no difference in the dye. Rather, the result or manifestation of the dyeing is altogether related to the quality of the fabric. Today the Spirit is like the dye. We all have been put into the Spirit, yet our manifestations are different. These differences are not due to the Holy Spirit whom we have received, because we all have the same Holy Spirit. Rather, the differences are due to us who are being dyed. This is related to the matter of our character.

The reason the apostle Paul could enjoy the Spirit of God as much as he did was because he had a good character and was diligent in all things. The brother in 1 Corinthians who had committed fornication undoubtedly had less enjoyment of the Holy Spirit because he had a poor character and was indifferent toward everything. The difference between these two people was not due to a difference in the Holy Spirit they had received but due to a difference in their character. The reason a person commits a fallen act is somewhat related to his character. Hence, those who truly love and pursue the Lord, not to mention those who serve and work for the Lord full time, must pay attention to the matter of character if they desire to live the Body life.

Many of the teachings of the Lord Jesus and of the apostles in the New Testament, beginning with Matthew, reveal the matter of our character, even though the word *character* is not used. You cannot inspire a piece of stone or motivate a piece of wood because neither has a living character. Character is a serious matter. The measure of grace we receive of the Lord and the degree to which the function of that grace is manifested are determined by the kind of character that we have. Therefore, the building up of our character is the most crucial matter in our service.

BEING EQUIPPED WITH THE TRUTH

Second, we need to be equipped with the truth. No one can serve the Lord without a proper knowledge of the truth. Paul said that we need to cut straight the word of the truth (2 Tim. 2:15). If we do not know the truth, how can we cut straight the word of the truth? Therefore, in order to serve the Lord we must pursue to know the truth and be equipped with the truth.

BEING FILLED WITH THE HOLY SPIRIT

The third fundamental matter in serving the Lord is having the Holy Spirit and being filled with the Holy Spirit.

The Divine Trinity

The Holy Spirit is the Spirit—the ultimate consummation of the Spirit of God and the ultimate expression of the processed, all-inclusive Triune God. This is a matter that

Christianity has not seen. God is triune. He is the Father, the Son, and the Spirit, yet They are not three separate persons. In eternity past, before He had passed through the process of incarnation, death, and resurrection, God was already triune. Using human words, we may say that in eternity past God was in His original state. For God to reach man, He must be triune. The Father is the source, the Son is the course, and the Spirit is the flow, the arriving, and the reaching.

The Holy Spirit is God reaching man. In the past God hid Himself in unapproachable light as the eternal Father (1 Tim. 6:16; James 1:17). When He was expressed, He was expressed as the Son (John 1:18). Now when He reaches man, He reaches man as the Spirit. This does not mean that there are three Gods or that the Father, the Son, and the Spirit are three separate persons. According to the teaching and revelation in the Scriptures, the Father, the Son, and the Spirit are distinct but not separate. Distinction is a matter of being, whereas separation is a matter of person. Theologically, it is difficult to determine the exact distinctions among the three of the Triune God. The question of how great the distinctions are among the three has never been easy to answer.

Hence, when we speak the truth concerning the Trinity, we have to be particularly cautious. We should avoid speaking too much lest we become presumptuous. In John 14 Philip asked the Lord to show them the Father. The Lord answered, "Have I been so long a time with you, and you have not known Me, Philip? He who has seen Me has seen the Father; how is it that you say, Show us the Father?" (vv. 8-9). This indicates that when the disciples saw the Son, they saw the Father. Where the Son was, there was the Father. The Lord Jesus' answer indicates that He was surprised by Philip's question. Suppose I am meeting with you, and you say to me, "Brother Lee, we would like to see Witness Lee." I would be shocked and would reply, "What are you talking about? Since I have been meeting with you, how could it be that you have not seen me? I am Witness Lee." This is what the Lord meant by His answer.

The doctrine concerning the Trinity is very mysterious and is not easy to preach. Most theological students do not study the Bible in a fine and thorough way. Instead, they are taught according to the traditional theological teachings. They receive the doctrine of the Trinity that was presented in the creed that was put out by the Council of Nicea. We cannot say that this kind of teaching in the seminaries is wrong, but such teaching is too rough and general. It is not detailed enough. The Nicene Creed was formulated in A.D. 325 at the Council of Nicea. Throughout the more than one thousand six hundred years since then, a great deal of research and development has been done concerning the doctrine of the Trinity, and this research and development has become a body of learning. With this learning as our foundation, we have studied this matter in a finer and deeper way.

When we released the result of our study in the United States, some theologians and professors came to us to debate with us, but in the end, they lost the debate because they had not studied thoroughly enough. They thought that they knew the truth well since they had received a theological education and had obtained doctoral degrees in theology. Actually, they did not understand the profound truths in the Bible at all. For example, some of them said that God is three and that the three of the Trinity are distinct and separate. In Orange County, Southern California, the opposers put out an unofficial pamphlet that clearly pointed out that according to their theology the Father, the Son, and the Spirit are distinct and separate. Therefore, I simply put out a message telling them that the Father, the Son, and the Spirit are distinct but not separate.

I pointed out that in the Gospel of John the Lord Jesus implicitly said, "I am in the Father and the Father is in Me" (14:10-11). He also said, "I and the Father are one" (10:30). Furthermore, He said, "He who sent Me is with Me; He has not left Me alone" (8:29). Thus, how could They be separate? After I put out such an article, none of the opposers would humbly admit their mistakes. Nevertheless, they were enlightened and were taught a lesson. Therefore, since that time, they have begun to say that the Three of the Trinity are distinct and no longer say that They are separate.

The Father, the Son, and the Spirit, though distinct, are

not separate. When the Lord Jesus said that he who had seen Him had seen the Father, what He meant was that the Son is the Father. His word also implied that the Son is in the Father, the Father is in the Son, and the Father and the Son are one. Since the Father and the Son are distinct, this indicates that They are two. We cannot say that since the Father and the Son are one, They are exactly the same. If They were exactly the same, there would not be any distinctions among the Father, the Son, and the Spirit. God would simply be one and would not be the Father, the Son, and the Spirit.

This is the most mysterious point concerning the person of God. Our God is God, yet He is also the Father, the Son, and the Spirit. He is one, yet He has the aspect of being three—the Father, the Son, and the Spirit. Even though He is the Father, the Son, and the Spirit, They are inseparable. Hence, over one thousand eight hundred years ago, those who studied the Bible were forced to invent the word *coinhere* to describe the Divine Trinity. The word *coinherence* is not emphasized in today's theology. Today's theology pays attention only to the word *coexistence,* because theologians used this word along with the Bible to defeat the heresy of modalism.

Modalism is also called Sabellianism. Because Sabellius was the leading exponent of modalism, his name was used to represent modalism. Modalism denies the coexistence of the Father, the Son, and the Spirit. It claims that God is one but not three. According to modalism, in the past God was the Father, and when He was manifested in the flesh, He became the Son. Once the Son came, the Father no longer existed, that is, once the Father became the Son, the Father ceased to exist. The Son existed on the earth for a period of time and then became the Holy Spirit, and once He became the Spirit, the Son also ceased to exist. Hence, according to modalism the Father, the Son, and the Spirit do not coexist. This is definitely a heresy. Today all the fundamental theologians believe in the Trinity, but the problem is that their speaking causes people to think that there are three Gods. This is because they focus on the aspect of God being three and neglect the aspect of God being one. Therefore, their understanding leans toward tritheism. Modalism emphasizes the aspect of God being one and neglects the aspect of God being three, thus becoming an extreme. Fundamental theology pays attention only to the aspect of the coexistence of the Father, the Son, and the Spirit and overlooks the aspect of Their coinherence, hence becoming another extreme.

Coinherence implies not only a simultaneous existence but also a simultaneous and mutual indwelling. It implies that the Father, the Son, and the Spirit do not exist separately but that They exist in the way of mutually indwelling one another simultaneously. The Son is in the Father, the Father is in the Son, the Father and the Son are in the Spirit, and the Spirit is also in the Father and the Son. This is the genuine Divine Trinity. An overemphasis of coexistence may lead to tritheism, and an overemphasis of God being one may lead to modalism. Both are extremes and are wrong. We believe in the Divine Trinity revealed in the Scriptures.

The Holy Spirit Being the Ultimate Consummation of the Triune God

In the Divine Trinity, the Father is the source, the Son is the course, the expression, and the Spirit is the flow, the reaching. Therefore, the Holy Spirit is the Triune God reaching us. When the Triune God reaches us, He is the Spirit. When we receive the Spirit, we receive the Triune God. This does not mean that when the Spirit comes, neither the Son nor the Father come. When the Spirit comes, the Triune God comes. The error of tritheism is that it asserts that when Jesus Christ came, He left the heavenly Father on the throne, and after He resurrected, ascended, and sat down at the right hand of God, He sent the Holy Spirit as His representative to enter into man. Hence, in 1967 we began to defend the truth concerning the Divine Trinity and published numerous messages to utterly expose the erroneous, heretical teachings concerning the Triune God.

We are fighting the battle for the truth with the Scripture as our basis. The heretical scholars do not study the Bible thoroughly. They say things based upon the limited knowledge they have obtained by studying only the traditional theology.

They despise me, considering me to be merely an old Chinese man. They are not willing to believe that although their Western missionaries went to China to teach the Bible to the Chinese and to preach to them, now there is a Chinese man coming to teach them. They are not willing to accept and believe this fact. They would not consider the fact that although they have studied theology a little, I have been studying the Bible in depth for sixty years and have put out quite a few books. When I fight, I can defeat them just by quoting a few verses from the Bible.

The truth concerning the Divine Trinity is that the Father is the source, the Son is the course, coming with the source, and the Spirit is the reaching, the flow, coming with the source. Hence, the Holy Spirit comes with both the Father and the Son. Today the Lord Jesus is not only sitting in heaven at the right hand of God but is also living in us. Galatians 2:20 says, "It is Christ who lives in me," and Colossians 1:27 says, "Christ in you, the hope of glory." Moreover, in Ephesians 3:17 Paul prayed that Christ would make His home in our hearts. It is wrong to say that Christ is in heaven but not in us. According to the pure truth of the Scriptures, Christ is not only dwelling and living in us, but He is also making His home in us.

Therefore, I invented several terms to explain the truth that is in the Scriptures. The Holy Spirit today is the processed, all-inclusive Spirit, the ultimate consummation of the Triune God. Today in the light of the Lord's recovery, the Spirit whom we enjoy and experience is the ultimate consummation of the Triune God.

The Process through Which
the Triune God Passed

Since there is a consummation, there must have been a process. First, God passed through incarnation. The One who was incarnated was not merely the Son but the entire Triune God, comprising the Father, the Son, and the Spirit. As proof of this matter, John 1:1 and 14 say, "In the beginning was the Word, and the Word was with God, and the Word was God....And the Word became flesh." The incarnated God is not just one-third of God but the Triune God in His entirety. Under the influence of traditional theology, most Christians believe that it was only the Son who was manifested in the flesh. Actually, the One who was incarnated is nothing less than the Triune God Himself.

Furthermore, when the Lord Jesus lived on the earth, it was not only the Son but the Triune God who was living on the earth. When the Lord Jesus died on the cross, it was not only the Son but the Triune God who passed through death. Acts 20:28 proves this point, saying, "The church of God, which He obtained through His own blood." Usually we refer to the blood as the precious blood of the Lord Jesus, but Paul says that it was God's blood. This shows that the One who died on the cross was not merely a man. He was also God; He was nothing less than the Triune God.

Therefore, it was the Triune God who was incarnated, who passed through human living, who died, and who resurrected. In resurrection, the Spirit came. This Spirit is the life-giving Spirit, the issue of the incarnated Triune God who passed through the process of death and resurrection (1 Cor. 15:45). In other words, the Spirit is the ultimate consummation and the ultimate expression of the processed Triune God.

Receiving the Ultimate Consummation of the Triune God

Hence, the New Testament shows that for us to receive the Spirit is to receive the ultimate consummation of the Triune God, that is, to receive the processed Triune God. Today the Holy Spirit is the processed Triune God. He is not the Triune God before incarnation but the Triune God who has passed through incarnation, human living, death, and resurrection. There are all kinds of riches in the Triune God—divinity, humanity, human living, the all-inclusive death, the all-conquering resurrection, the all-transcending ascension, and the all-receiving descension. Today the Spirit is moving in the universe for man to receive Him. This gospel is truly great!

Genesis 1 reveals that prior to God's restoration of the heavens and the earth, the Spirit of God brooded upon the surface of the waters (v. 2). This Spirit was the Triune God but not the ultimate consummation of the Triune God, the all-inclusive Spirit, or the processed Triune God. The Spirit in Genesis 1 had only the element of divinity and not the elements of humanity, human living, death, resurrection, or ascension. He was the "raw" Triune God, the initial expression of the Triune God. However, the Spirit who is moving in the universe today is different from the Spirit in Genesis 1. This does not mean that there are two Spirits. They are the same one Spirit, but this Spirit has been processed. The Spirit in the beginning was the initial expression of the Triune God, and the Spirit at the consummation is the ultimate expression of the Triune God. Today the Spirit whom we receive is the Spirit in Genesis 1 who has been processed and consummated.

In the past there was a co-worker in Hong Kong who was against me because I said that the Christ in Revelation is different from the Christ in the Gospel of John. Indeed, the Christ in the Gospel of John and the Christ in Revelation are different, but this does not mean that there are two Christs. When John saw the Christ whom he wrote about in the Gospel of John, he was not afraid of Him and even reclined on His breast (13:25). The same John saw the Christ whom he described in the book of Revelation. This occurred several decades later, by which time John was already old and was not afraid to suffer or die. However, when he saw Christ this time, he was frightened, and he fell at His feet as dead (1:17). Moreover, the Christ in the Gospel of John had two eyes, but the Christ in Revelation has seven eyes (5:6). Then how can we say that the Christ in the Gospel of John is the same as the Christ in Revelation? We surely cannot say that the Christ in the Gospel of John and the Christ in Revelation are the same. But the fact that the Christ in the Gospel of John and the Christ in Revelation are different does not mean that the Christ in the Gospel of John and the Christ in Revelation are two different persons. Rather, the Christ in the Gospel of John and the Christ in Revelation are still one and the same.

In the same way, we do not say that there are two Holy Spirits. What we say is that the one Holy Spirit is different dispensationally. In Genesis 1, the Holy Spirit was in the initial stage and had not passed through a process. In Revelation, however, the Holy Spirit is no longer in the initial stage. He is in the highest and ultimate stage and has become the seven Spirits (1:4; 4:5; 5:6). The seven Spirits are not seven individual Spirits but one Spirit intensified sevenfold.

Being Filled with the Consummated Spirit

God has already created the heavens and the earth, become flesh, and passed through human living on the earth for thirty-three and a half years. Moreover, He has gone through death, dying on the cross in seven statuses, and He has resurrected, ascended, and descended. Today He is on the throne and also in us, and He is also operating in the whole world. Hence, whenever we go to preach the gospel, we can tell people that the Word is near them, in their mouth and in their heart (Rom. 10:8). The Word is Christ, and Christ is the Spirit. The Spirit is like the air, which is in our mouth and within us. Like the air, the Spirit is also in our mouth and within us. Today our God is such a wonderful One. He is our Savior and our life, and He is also the Spirit. We need to be filled with such a Spirit.

In Galatians 3 the Spirit is referred to as the blessing of the gospel. The gospel that we preach contains a central blessing—the Spirit—which was promised by God to Abraham from the beginning (v. 8). As early as four thousand years ago, God promised to bless Abraham. This blessing was to be the Triune God incarnated to be the seed of Abraham, and it was in this seed, who is Christ, that all the nations would be blessed (vv. 14, 16). How could Christ as the seed become a blessing to the nations? It was by His passing through a process. He lived a human life and then went to the cross, where He accomplished an all-inclusive death and dealt with all the problems among men and all the problems between God and man. Then He resurrected to become the life-giving Spirit as the consummation of the Triune God. It is this life-giving Spirit as the consummation of the Triune God who is moving on the earth today to be a blessing to all the people in the world.

Hence, this Spirit is the gospel, the salvation, and the very God Himself, Jesus Christ our Savior. He is our life and power. Essentially, He is in us as life, and economically, He is upon us as power. It is this Spirit whom we preach, and it is this Spirit whom we have believed in, received, and obtained. Galatians 3:2 says that we have received the Spirit. Moreover, Ephesians 1:13 says, "In whom you also, having heard the word of the truth, the gospel of your salvation, in Him also believing, you were sealed with the Holy Spirit of the promise." At the time we were saved, the Holy Spirit, who is God Himself, entered into us as a seal to mark us out, indicating that we belong to God. This indicates that the Spirit whom we have received is in reality the Triune God Himself.

Now what we need is to be filled with this Spirit. In Ephesians 5:18 Paul exhorts us to be filled in spirit. We need to be filled in spirit with the Spirit—the all-inclusive, life-giving Spirit as the consummation of the processed Triune God. How can we be filled with such a Spirit? We can be filled through prayer and the confession of our sins, which includes repentance. On the day of Pentecost, after the people had heard the gospel and had been touched, they asked Peter what they had to do in order to be saved. Peter told them, "Repent and each one of you be baptized upon the name of Jesus Christ for the forgiveness of your sins, and you will receive the gift of the Holy Spirit" (Acts 2:38). This shows us that as long as we fulfill the principle of repenting, confessing our sins, and thoroughly dealing with our sins, we will definitely receive the Holy Spirit. Just as we initially received the Holy Spirit and were saved through repentance and confession, today we also receive the filling of the Holy Spirit through repentance and confession.

We experience regeneration and salvation once for all, but we need to repent and confess our sins day by day throughout our whole life. For example, consider our washing of our hands. We do not wash our hands once after we are born and then have no need to wash them again. Rather, we have to wash our hands many times a day throughout our lifetime. Another example is breathing. We cannot cease breathing just because we took a deep breath once. Rather, we have to breathe unceasingly to preserve our life. Breathing is like our prayer, and hand-washing is like our confession. If we want to be filled with the Holy Spirit, we must pray and confess every day.

Today the processed Triune God has been consummated as the all-inclusive Spirit. People in the Pentecostal movement assert that in order to receive the Holy Spirit Christians must fast or do certain things until they hear a big noise and open their mouths and speak in tongues. This is altogether nonsense. After the Triune God accomplished redemption, He became the life-giving Spirit, and, like the air, He is in our mouth and in our heart. Whenever we open our mouth and call on the Lord's name, we receive the Holy Spirit and are saved (Rom. 10:8-13). However, after our salvation we still have to be filled with the Holy Spirit through our daily prayer and confession.

We need to confess our sins thoroughly, especially before we go to contact people or prophesy for the Lord in the meetings. When we pray and confess our sins to a certain degree, we will be filled with the Holy Spirit inwardly. We do not need to analyze whether it is the essential Spirit or the economical Spirit, because the two are just one Spirit. Although there is a distinction between the essential Spirit and the economical Spirit in function, They are still the same one Spirit.

Secrets to Maintaining the Filling of the Holy Spirit

Not Quenching the Spirit

After we have been filled with the Holy Spirit, we still have to do a few things to maintain the filling. First, we should not quench the Spirit (1 Thes. 5:19). The Spirit causes us to be burning in spirit (Rom. 12:11) and also causes us to fan into flame the gift which is in us (2 Tim. 1:6). Hence, we should not quench the Spirit.

Not Grieving the Holy Spirit

Second, we should not grieve the Holy Spirit (Eph. 4:30). To grieve the Holy Spirit is to displease Him and to not walk according to Him in our daily living (Rom. 8:4). How do we know when the Holy Spirit is grieved? We can know by our living. If we are not joyful in our Christian life, this is a sign that the Holy Spirit is grieving in us. It is because the Holy Spirit is grieving in us that we are not joyful. If we are joyful, this indicates that the Holy Spirit in us is also joyful. A sister testified that she once had prayed to the extent that her whole being was refreshed, light-hearted, and so full of joy. This is proof that the Holy Spirit in her was joyful. Hence, to not grieve the Holy Spirit is to not grieve yourself.

Obeying the Holy Spirit

Third, on the positive side, we must obey the Holy Spirit. In Acts 5 Peter said, "The Holy Spirit, whom God has given to those who obey Him" (v. 32). This shows that the Holy Spirit is for us to obey. Obedience is the way and the requirement for us to enjoy the Holy Spirit. Romans 8:4 says, "Do not walk according to the flesh but according to the spirit." This is the way to be filled with the Holy Spirit and the requirement for maintaining a life of being filled with the Holy Spirit. We should not only study these verses but also put them into practice in our daily life.

Paying Attention to the Filling of the Holy Spirit

Today in the church life there is an urgent need for the filling of the Holy Spirit. Without the filling of the Holy Spirit, we lack vigor and vitality. Without vitality, we will become deadened, like a deflated tire. Today in the changing of our system we are practicing the God-ordained way to have a balance between big meetings and small meetings so that everyone can function organically. This is right. However, if the saints are not vital or vigorous in the church life, then our efforts to change the system will be futile. Today in the church life, we still lack the filling of the Holy Spirit. For this reason, I hope that all of you young people would take the lead to pay attention to the filling of the Holy Spirit and pursue to be filled with the Holy Spirit every day.

People in the Pentecostal movement speak in tongues in a miraculous way, thinking that this is the only way to receive the Holy Spirit. This is absolutely erroneous. No doubt, when the Holy Spirit was outpoured in Acts, there was truly the speaking in tongues. However, of all the Epistles, only 1 Corinthians mentions the matter of speaking in tongues, and the word there is an adjustment, a correction, and a restriction on the negative side. Speaking in tongues is not mentioned in the Epistles as a requirement for being filled with the Holy Spirit. Rather, the requirements are repentance, confession of sins, not quenching the Spirit, not grieving the Holy Spirit, obeying the Holy Spirit, and walking according to the spirit in all things.

Casting Out Demons and Healing

You must reject what is taught in the Pentecostal movement. Do not speak in tongues, because once you speak in tongues, your spiritual life will be slain. However, there are a few matters which you should not refuse but should pay attention to in your practice, especially when you go to preach the gospel in the villages. These are the matters concerning healing and casting out demons, which you must do by walking according to the spirit. Do not say that you cannot do these things, because it is not you who can but the Lord Jesus, the Spirit, who can. You have to cast out demons in the name of the Lord Jesus and by relying on the power of His precious blood. All demons are afraid of these two things. When you cast out a demon, the first sentence you must say is, "The precious blood of Christ Jesus covers me." Then you must tell the troubling demon, "Under the precious blood of Jesus I cast you out in His name." In this way, the demon will have to obey and leave.

There are not that many demons in the large cities, but there are many in the villages. The demons will grasp the opportunity to trouble the ignorant people and to possess their bodies whenever they are ill or injured. Thus, when you go to the villages, you cannot avoid the matter of casting out demons. From now on, all the workers among us must be ready to deliberately cast out demons whenever the occasion requires. Moreover, you must heal people's sicknesses when necessary. You do not need to worry about whether or not you can heal the disease. You simply need to do it by faith. However, do not hold healing meetings like those in the Pentecostal movement. The Lord does not want us to do this. Rather, the Lord wants us to cast out every demon and heal every disease when we preach the gospel in the villages.

There is a brother among us who can heal diseases and cast out demons. One time he cast out a demon by writing the sentence, "Jehovah sent Jesus as the Savior, and Jesus casts out demons." Then he asked the demon-possessed person to read it and to call on the Lord. The next day, that person testified that the demon had left him. This may seem to be a joke, but this is actually the right way. Our way to cast out demons is to ask people to read the Lord's Word and to call on the Lord's name continuously. Once a person is saved, the demon will leave him.

About twenty years ago in mainland China, Christians who preached the gospel in the villages would encounter situations that required them to cast out demons and heal diseases. Fifty years ago there was a book concerning demon possession. The author was a Western missionary from a Presbyterian church. While he was preaching the gospel in my hometown of Chefoo, he had many experiences of casting out demons. He recorded all these experiences in detail. Mrs. Penn-Lewis also mentioned her experiences of this matter in *The War on the Saints*. When I saw this book, I wanted to buy it. Later I bought it in Shanghai at a bookstore that exclusively sold used spiritual books written by Western missionaries. Today when we go out to preach the gospel, we must meet this need. The way to meet this need is not to hold tongue-speaking or healing meetings but to pursue the filling of the Holy Spirit and to remain filled with the Holy Spirit. Then we may cast out every demon and heal every disease that we encounter. This is the proper practice.

Prayer: Lord, fill us with Your Holy Spirit. We do not want to merely have knowledge. We desire to be full of the Holy Spirit, full of the Triune God. Lord, we thank You for being the processed Triune God supplying us in our spirit. Every day we want to exercise to be filled with the Holy Spirit through prayer and confession. We do not want to quench the

Spirit or to grieve the Holy Spirit but to obey the Spirit and to walk according to the spirit so that we may be full of the Spirit in our daily life.

Lord Jesus, we want to daily build up ourselves under Your precious blood and in Your name to meet the need in Your move. We praise You that on the cross You have already destroyed the devil, who has the might of death. Now as the life-giving Spirit You are making that which You accomplished on the cross a reality in us. Lord, remember us and cause that which You accomplished to become our living so that our living would be without sin and without death. Lord, we want to confess our sins every day and to cast out all the demons for the coming of the kingdom of God.

Lord, shine on us and cleanse us daily that we may become vessels unto honor and be completely filled with the Holy Spirit. Lord, draw us each day that we may be Your witnesses in our living. Amen.

CHAPTER ELEVEN

LEARNING THE SECRET TO READING THE BIBLE

READING THE BIBLE IN THE WAY OF HITTING THE MARK

In reading the Bible you need to learn to find the main points and the general thought. When you read the Bible, you must learn to hit the mark. For example, when you eat chicken, you should eat its meat and not pay attention to its feathers, skin, and bones. Chicken feathers, skin, and bones are essential to the growth of a chicken, for without them it would not be possible for a chicken to exist. When you eat chicken, however, you should eat only its meat. Let us use a fish as another example. A fish has a head, a tail, fins, and bones. To properly enjoy a fish, you have to know which parts to eat. Many Americans do not know which parts of a fish can be eaten, so they discard the fish head, the fish tail, and the fish bones. As a result, they do not get the proper enjoyment of the fish. When we read the Bible, we must learn to hit the mark. Whether or not we do this depends on whether or not we are focused on the main points and have the proper enjoyment.

The authors of the Bible did not include only "chicken meat" when they wrote the Scriptures. They included geography, history, and various people, matters, and events. When we read the Scriptures, however, we should not focus on these items; instead, we should endeavor to find the main points pertaining to life and spiritual principles, such as the meaning of salvation and the meaning of grace. After reading a particular section of the Scriptures, we should also try to speak the main points and understand the outline of that section. You who are learning to work for the Lord must learn how to speak properly. You must not only speak properly when giving a message, you must also speak in a logical and attractive way that is full of content when you are conversing with people one on one.

A SUMMARY OF PHILIPPIANS 1

Let us use Philippians 1 as an illustration of how we should read the Bible. You may have studied this chapter very well; that is, you may have endeavored to grasp the main point and to find the central line. As a result, you may know that the subject of this chapter is living Christ for His magnification. You greatly miss the mark, however, if you do not see the matter of the bountiful supply of the Spirit of Jesus Christ (v. 19). Without the Spirit, how can you live Christ? Without the Spirit, how can Christ be magnified in you? The key, the life-pulse, to live Christ and to magnify Him is the bountiful supply of the Spirit of Jesus Christ. Without the bountiful supply of the Spirit of Jesus Christ, you also will not have the power to defend the gospel.

Paul clearly pointed out that his defense of the gospel, his preaching of the gospel, his suffering of persecution, and even his imprisonment all resulted in his living Christ for His magnification and all hinged on the bountiful supply of the Spirit of Jesus Christ. We can use the breath in our human body to illustrate the importance of the Spirit. If our human body has all its parts and organs intact but does not have breath within, it will be a corpse. We can also use the gas in a car as an illustration. A cheap, old car with gas is better than the best car without gas. The bountiful supply of the Spirit of Jesus Christ is the "breath" and the "gas" for our experience of Christ. The bountiful supply of the Spirit of Jesus Christ is the life-pulse of Philippians 1.

A chicken has feathers, skin, bones, and meat. This is obvious, and we know that we should eat the chicken meat. But when we read the Bible, it is not so easy to find the "chicken meat." This is the preciousness of reading the Bible. Philippians chapter one has thirty verses, and every letter of every word is of the same size and style. Moreover, the phrase *the bountiful supply of the Spirit of Jesus Christ* is not printed in large or bold type. Hence, when we read the Bible, it is up to us to find this phrase, to magnify it, and to apply it in our daily life. Reading the Bible may be likened to responding to a traffic signal. When we see a traffic signal, we know that we have to stop at a red light and proceed at a green light. Likewise, when we read the Bible, we have to find the life-pulse, the most precious point, of the portion that we are reading.

The entire book of Philippians is concerned with the experience of Christ. In particular, chapter one speaks on the experience of Christ in several aspects. First, it mentions the defense of the gospel. Regardless of how others preached or what they preached, Paul still preached the proper gospel. In doing this he lived Christ. For the preaching of the proper gospel, he was persecuted and even put in prison, yet he still lived Christ that Christ would be magnified in him. How could Paul defend the gospel, preach the proper gospel, and live Christ in a proper way so as to magnify Christ even to the extent that he did not care about being imprisoned? The key, the life-pulse, for him to do this was the bountiful supply of the Spirit of Jesus Christ. When we read Philippians 1 we should make note of this fact and summarize this chapter in this way.

The whole book of Philippians is about the experience of Christ. Chapter one tells us that in order to experience Christ, we need to defend the gospel, to preach the proper gospel in a proper way, and to even suffer persecution for the gospel's sake. We need to always live Christ that Christ may be magnified in us. The key, the secret, and the life-pulse to doing this is the bountiful supply of the Spirit of Jesus Christ.

The way to apply the bountiful supply of the Spirit of Jesus Christ is through prayer. Verse 19 of chapter one says, "For I know that for me this will turn out to salvation through your petition and the bountiful supply of the Spirit of Jesus Christ." Here salvation does not mean that Paul would be rescued from the prison. It means that he would be delivered from the failure of not living Christ. In the midst of persecution and imprisonment he would still live Christ, defend the gospel, and magnify Christ. Paul was able to continue to preach the proper gospel and to defend the gospel even during his imprisonment. Thus, he lived Christ and magnified Christ. This was his salvation. How could he be saved in this way? It was through the petition of the saints and the bountiful supply of the Spirit of Jesus Christ. After the saints prayed for him, the Spirit supplied him, and once he was supplied, he was saved, so that instead of being defeated, he was strong and able to preach the gospel, defend the gospel, suffer persecution, live Christ, and allow Christ to be magnified in him as always whether through life or through death. This is a crystallized exposition of Philippians 1.

A SUMMARY OF GALATIANS 1

Let us take Galatians 1 as another example of how to read the Bible. In the beginning of Galatians, Paul says, "Who [Christ] gave Himself for our sins that He might rescue us out of the present evil age according to the will of our God and Father" (v. 4). What Paul means in this verse is that Christ died for our sins to accomplish redemption that He might rescue us not out of sin, as is commonly thought, but out of the evil age. The evil age here refers particularly to the religious world. Then Paul continued to say that the gospel he preached was received through a revelation (v. 12). This is in contrast to the teachings of religion, which come from tradition. Galatians 6:14-15 proves that the evil age denotes the religious world. The second half of chapter one also proves this. In verses 13 and 14 Paul says, "For you have heard of my manner of life formerly in Judaism....And I advanced in Judaism beyond many contemporaries in my race, being more abundantly a zealot for the traditions of my fathers." Judaism is a religion, and one receives this religion by receiving its traditions.

The gospel preached by Paul was received through revelation and not through tradition. Paul said, "It pleased God...to reveal His Son in me" (vv. 15-16). The focus of the revelation that Paul received was Christ, the Son of God. Hence, Galatians clearly shows us that Christ is versus religion. It is a fact that Christ died for us that we might be delivered from the religious world. However, how can we be delivered? How does Christ rescue us? His death alone was not enough to deliver us. He needed also to be resurrected. Through His death and resurrection Christ became the life-giving Spirit (1 Cor. 15:45b). When this life-giving Spirit, who is the living Christ, is revealed in us, He rescues us out of religion. The living Christ comes into us not by tradition and heredity but by revelation. Christ is versus religion. The center, the focus, of the revelation that we receive from God is the living Christ.

How do we know that Christ is the living Christ? We know this because He can enter into us and be revealed in us. The living Christ, who is revealed in us and is versus religion, rescues us from the religious world. How does He come into us? He comes into us not through our heritage or tradition but through revelation—God reveals His Son in us. Religion is a matter of tradition; Christ is a matter of revelation. This is a summary of Galatians 1.

LEARNING FROM MISTAKES AND FAILURES

In order to study the Bible in this way, you must learn a secret—to practice continuously. You should not be afraid of your shortages in learning or in training, and you should not say that you are not well educated or adequately trained. You must simply grasp every opportunity to practice, and you must continuously endeavor to learn to speak. If you do this, you will do well. You should not be afraid of your lack in studying the Bible. You should be afraid only of pretending that you have thoroughly studied the Bible when you have not. If you pretend in this way, it is as if you are hanging yourself. In every training meeting there is a testing. During these tests, you should not be afraid but should actively participate. This is a training. If you do not answer properly, and I criticize you, this will profit you more than your personal Bible reading. In addition, everyone else will receive help as well. When you sacrifice yourself and receive criticism, everyone will receive benefit, but the one who will receive the most benefit is you. You should not think to yourself, "If I speak, the first time I speak I must speak so well that everyone will be greatly impressed. If I am unable to do this, I will not speak at all." If you were able to speak in such a way, then you would not need this training.

The secret to being trained is to be unafraid of making mistakes, of failing, of falling short, and of having your weaknesses exposed. If you write a composition perfectly, when your teacher reads it, you will not benefit. However, if your composition is written poorly and your teacher adjusts it, you will have the opportunity to learn a great deal. The more mistakes you make, the more you will learn. In the same way, when you are in the training, you have to try your best to expose your mistakes so that you can receive the benefit. Do not expect to speak excellently. Good students are those who intentionally hide their talents and knowledge and allow their weak points to be manifested so that they can receive instruction from their teachers. When I was young, I learned English very well. Later when I went to an English college founded by some Americans, I could have almost taught the teachers, so the principal agreed that I could be exempt from taking English classes. Since you come here to be trained, unless you think that you are better than your teachers and can be exempt, you have to learn in a serious way.

THE FILLING OF THE HOLY SPIRIT

In this message we want to see something further concerning the filling of the Holy Spirit. From the very beginning of the Lord's recovery among us, we have paid much attention to the filling of the Holy Spirit. We have been enlightened to see that there is more to the Holy Spirit than what is taught in Christian theology. We see that the Spirit is the ultimate expression of the processed Triune God. In this ultimate expression, there is divinity, humanity, human living, Christ's all-inclusive death and its effectiveness, resurrection and its power, ascension, and descension. The Holy Spirit is an all-inclusive, compound, life-giving, and consummated Spirit. Therefore, the Spirit is exceedingly rich.

In the past even though we spoke so much about the filling of the Holy Spirit, it seemed that the saints were not paying much attention to this matter. Last year when I came back to Taiwan, I noticed that you all had learned to speak about the essential Spirit and the economical Spirit. However, although you pay attention to the essential Spirit and the economical Spirit, you are still not filled with the Spirit. Hence, you lack the experience of the Spirit both essentially and economically. You have to know that regardless of how true it is that the Spirit has an essential aspect and an economical aspect, if you are not filled with Him, He cannot be the Spirit in you essentially nor the Spirit upon you economically. To experience the Spirit essentially and economically requires you to be filled with the Spirit.

In the table of contents of our hymnal, the first category is the blessing of the Trinity, the second is the worship of the Father, the third is the praise of the Lord, and the fourth is the fullness of the Spirit. In the category on the fullness of the Spirit, more than half of the hymns were written by me. There is a hymn in the Chinese hymnal that says that everything related to the relationship between God and man depends upon the Spirit. The strangest thing is that although I have given you such wonderful assets, no one has made use of them. Even my co-workers do not use these things in their work. I am afraid that a person can get saved and be among us for a long time and yet never hear a message about the filling of the Holy Spirit. The truth concerning the filling of the Holy Spirit is like a smoking flax among us. This is a great loss. Therefore, we must fan this fire into flame.

PURSUING THE FILLING OF THE HOLY SPIRIT

We have focused very much on the Spirit since the beginning of the Lord's recovery among us. We have not focused on a simple Spirit but on the consummated Spirit. Our co-workers have been taught a great deal and have been going out to work, but they lack the revelation of the Holy Spirit, and they do not emphasize the Holy Spirit. Take for example Galatians 1 and Philippians 1. Many of us do not see the meaning of the expression *to reveal His Son in me,* and many also do not grasp the significance of the phrase *the bountiful supply of the Spirit of Jesus Christ.* When you neglect these things, you miss too much. Similarly, although we have been working all the time, we have missed a crucial point—the filling of the Holy Spirit. Now we must go back to be rekindled in this matter. When you trainees are learning to serve the Lord, you must pursue to be filled with the Holy Spirit from the outset.

In *The Experience of Life,* the title of chapter fourteen is "Being Filled with the Holy Spirit." *Fundamental Truths in the Scriptures* also covers this truth. Our present burden is that you would pay attention to the daily filling of the Holy Spirit. Just as you cannot graduate from breathing after having breathed for one day, so also you cannot graduate from being filled with the Holy Spirit after having been filled once. You must be filled with the Holy Spirit day by day. This matter can never be over-emphasized. When you baptize people, you have be filled with the Holy Spirit. Otherwise, your baptism of them will deaden them. John the Baptist baptized people with water. The water buried and terminated them. The Lord Jesus baptized people with the Spirit and into the Spirit (Matt. 3:11). The Spirit enlivened them. Hence, you not only need to lead people to receive the baptism in water so that they may be buried and terminated, but you also need to help them to receive the baptism in the Spirit so that they may be made alive. You have to pay attention to this point and preach these two baptisms in a proper way especially when you go out to labor on the campuses.

MOVING BY THE FILLING OF THE HOLY SPIRIT

Today in Christianity when people are baptized, whether by sprinkling or by immersion, they are often baptized with water but without the Spirit. Although the Pentecostals stress the Spirit, they have only the name and do not have much of the reality. We must be a group of people who genuinely pay attention to the Spirit and fan the Spirit into flame. The Bible records that even the Lord Jesus needed to be filled with the Holy Spirit. Luke 4:1 says, "Jesus, full of the Holy Spirit." Hence, from now on we all have to pay attention to this matter. Before people set off for a long trip, they have to make sure that their car is filled up with gas and that their tires are fully filled with air. Likewise, before we go out to speak for the Lord and contact people one on one, we must pray thoroughly so that we will be filled with the Spirit as our "gas" and our "air." The Holy Spirit is our gas and our air, filling us so that we can move.

I say again, when you go out, you have to cast out demons whenever necessary and without consideration. Consideration is a sign of lack of faith. Even if you feel that you do not have faith, you have to pray immediately to ask the Lord for faith. Then you must cast out the demons in the Lord's name. In Matthew 12:28, the Lord Jesus said, "But if I, by the Spirit of God, cast out the demons, then the kingdom of God has come upon you." Here it mentions two matters—casting out the demons by the Holy Spirit and ushering in the kingdom of God by casting out the demons. Thus, when you go to the campuses and communities today, and when you go to the villages in the future, you have to cast out demons by the Holy Spirit to bring in the kingdom of God. This requires you to always be filled with the Holy Spirit.

It is relatively easy to cast out demons, but it is not that easy to heal diseases. Demons are easy to deal with. Once you apply the Lord's precious blood, you are covered, and once you employ the Lord's name, the demon is cast out. But you may not be able to heal a disease instantly. If someone asks you to lay hands on him, you cannot refuse him. You have to lay hands on him and pray for him that the Lord will heal him. However, you should not quickly lay hands on everyone who is sick. Paul said, "Lay hands quickly on no man" (1 Tim. 5:22). If you lay hands on every sick one, you are looking for trouble. You must cast out the demons whenever you encounter them; however, when you encounter sickness, you should lay hands on the sick only if you have been asked to do so. If you pursue the filling of the Holy Spirit, you will be able to cast out the demons and heal diseases.

The first thing that we must pay attention to is the filling of the Holy Spirit. Then, once we are filled with the Spirit, we should cast out demons and heal the sick. We do not care, however, for tongue-speaking or any strange miracles or wonders. People in the Pentecostal movement often do these things. This is a mistake. Gradually, those who get involved in

these things give them up. The infilling of the Holy Spirit is
the scientific way, and it is the truth revealed in the Scriptures. Today when you go out to preach the gospel, you have
to be filled with the Holy Spirit, then you have to cast out
demons and heal diseases. This is a law. In the past when we
preached the gospel, we merely paid attention to speaking
and did not rely on being filled with the Holy Spirit. Hence,
we also neglected healing and the casting out of demons. The
preaching of the gospel requires speaking, but in our words
there must be the Spirit, with whom is the power to cast out
demons and heal the sick. The Spirit is the power of the
gospel. If we preach the gospel in such a way, our gospel will
be powerful.

The New Testament reveals that in our preaching of the
gospel, we must have the Word (Rom. 10:14-15) and the Spirit
(Luke 24:49; Acts 1:4; 2:4). With the Word is the supply of life,
and with the Spirit is the power to cast out demons and to
heal (Acts 5:12-16; 16:18). If we have the Word and the Spirit,
our gospel will be powerful, and our work will be living and
effective. If you do not pursue the infilling of the Holy Spirit, I
am afraid that when you go out to baptize people, everyone
whom you baptize will become dead. Consequently, they will
neither attend the meetings nor pursue the Lord. If you want
to make people alive through baptism, you need to baptize
them not only in water but also in the Spirit. This means that
when you baptize people, you have to lead them to be filled
with the Holy Spirit. The way to do this is to teach them to
confess their sins, to pray, and to open themselves to receive
the infilling of the Holy Spirit.

Baptism is the first step a person must take after he has
believed in the Lord. Then he has to pursue the filling of the
Holy Spirit and to live and move by being filled with the Holy
Spirit. This is the proper living of a baptized person. The key
to being filled with the Holy Spirit lies in thoroughly confessing, praying, and opening ourselves. In the past we focused on
burying people in the water so that they would be delivered
from the world through the death of Christ. However, we did
not raise them up. As a result, they were still dead in spiritual matters, having neither spiritual "air" nor spiritual "gas"

because they were not filled with the Spirit. Now we must pay attention to helping people to be filled with the Holy Spirit, and we ourselves should also be such people.

Prayer: Lord, cause us to touch the key point and the central line so that we may be here solidly pursuing the filling of the Holy Spirit and exercising to be filled with the Holy Spirit, so that we may have the Word and the Spirit, so that we may bring people to be put to death and to receive life, and so that our gospel may be full of power. Lord, we not only receive this view, but we ask You to enable us to exercise and practice. Through our thorough confessions and prayers, cause us to open ourselves to You that we may be filled with the Holy Spirit and bring others to be filled with the Holy Spirit, so that we may bear Your testimony in our living and move. Amen.

Chapter Twelve

THE TRUTH CONCERNING
THE FILLING OF THE HOLY SPIRIT
AND THE PRACTICAL EXERCISE
TO BUILD UP OUR CHARACTER

OUR EMPHASIS BEING ON THE HOLY SPIRIT

Hymns, #212 in the Chinese hymnal was written based on the spiritual vision in Ezekiel 1 concerning four things—the wind, the cloud, the fire, and the electrum. If you read *The Visions of Ezekiel,* you will understand the meaning of this hymn. *Hymns,* #250, which is comparatively simple and easy to understand, was written based on Numbers 21:16-17. Stanza three says, "I will dig by praying, / Dig the dirt entirely, / Thus release the Spirit, / Let the stream flow freely." To say that we "will dig by praying" to "release the Spirit" may sound rather strange. It is common that we obtain water by digging a well, but how can we get the Spirit by digging? This matter is both wonderful and mysterious.

I wrote both these hymns in 1961. This strongly proves that we have put much emphasis on the filling of the Spirit since very early in our history. In the table of contents of our hymnal, the fourth category is "Fullness of the Spirit." The Chinese hymnal lists the following headings under this category—"As the Spirit of Reality," "As the Indwelling Spirit," "As the Spirit of Jesus Christ," "As the Comforter," "As the Spirit of Gifts," "As the Spirit of Life," "As the Living Water," "As the Fire," "As the Breath," "As the Wind," "As the Ointment (the Anointing)," "The Filling," "The Baptism," "The Two Aspects (the Spirit of Life and the Spirit of Power)," and "By the Cross." There are over thirty hymns in this category, and I wrote more than half of them. In Christianity there are only a small number of hymns on the Spirit, and the truth in these hymns is unclear and vague.

From this we can see that even since the beginning of the Lord's recovery among us, we paid much attention to the matter of the Spirit in the New Testament. The New Testament contains a great revelation concerning the Lord Jesus Christ. But the only way for Christ to be realized in a practical way in the believers' living and experience is through the Spirit. The Spirit is the realization of Christ. Hence, the Spirit is mentioned in every book of the New Testament. Moreover, in his Epistles Paul repeatedly refers to the Spirit and to our spirit. In Romans 8:16 He says, "The Spirit Himself witnesses with our spirit that we are children of God," and in 1 Corinthians 6:17 he writes, "He who is joined to the Lord is one spirit." Paul makes a particular point to connect these two spirits together. However, even Christian groups that are orthodox, such as the Baptist Church, do not dare to say much about the Spirit. Although the people in the Pentecostal movement do speak about the Spirit, they neglect this truth. In fact, they have made the matter of the Spirit difficult for people to understand because their speaking is without proper discernment and is often rather foolish.

Thank the Lord that when He raised us up over sixty years ago, we began to pay much attention to the Spirit. We particularly paid attention to this matter in all of our reading of the Bible. We also focused on this matter when we studied church history and read others' writings. Then based on our knowledge of the Bible, the help that we received from the writings of others, and our own research, we have published many books concerning the Spirit. Our hymnal is an excellent example of this. However, over the past twenty years, I still feel we have neglected this. This lack is most manifest in Taiwan and Southeast Asia. To neglect the matter of the Spirit is a great mistake.

For this reason we are endeavoring to change the basic form and way that we meet in the church and are focusing on our propagation. This is the change of system that we are trying to implement. The way for the church to propagate and for us to have an increase in numbers is to spread the gospel widely, and the secret for us to be able to do this is the filling of the Spirit. Hence, at this critical juncture, I hope that you young people will pursue the filling of the Holy Spirit so that your gospel may be powerful.

OUR GOD BEING ALTOGETHER A MATTER OF SPIRIT

The substance, the essence, of our God is Spirit. The Bible says that God is Spirit (John 4:24), love (1 John 4:8, 16), and light (1:5). In depicting God's nature, the New Testament emphasizes only three things—God is Spirit, God is love, and God is light. Regarding these three matters, note 3 of 1 John 1:5 in the New Testament Recovery Version says, "Spirit denotes the nature of God's person; love, the nature of God's essence; and light, the nature of God's expression." God Himself is a person, and with this person there is an essence and an expression. The nature of God's person is Spirit, the nature of God's essence is love, and the nature of God's expression is light. God Himself is Spirit, and the third person in His Trinity is the Holy Spirit. Moreover, He became the life-giving Spirit after passing through the processes of incarnation, human living, death, and resurrection. This shows us that the story of our God is altogether a story of the Spirit.

We need to know at least three things concerning God—first, God's substance is Spirit; second, the ultimate consummation of the person of the Divine Trinity is the Spirit; and third, God became flesh, passed through various processes, and eventually entered into resurrection to become the life-giving Spirit, who includes the elements of His divinity and His humanity, plus His incarnation, human living, death, resurrection, and ascension. These three items are like three steps. The first step is concerning God's substance; the second is concerning God's person; and the third is concerning His ultimate expression after passing through all the processes. These three steps, or layers, are all related to the Spirit—the substance of God is Spirit; the ultimate expression of His person is the Spirit; and after He became flesh and passed through various processes, His ultimate expression is still the

Spirit, the life-giving Spirit. This is the God who is revealed
in the New Testament. He is such a Spirit.

THE SPIRIT WITH OUR HUMAN SPIRIT

For us to experience the Spirit, the New Testament points
to our human spirit. We also stress this point. In our hymnal
we even have a hymn concerning the two spirits—*Hymns,*
#11. It is in the category "Worship of the Father." This hymn
says,

> 1 Thou, Father, who art Spirit true,
>   The holiest of all;
>   We worship in the spirit now,
>   In truth upon Thee call.

> 2 A spirit Thou hast made for us
>   That we may worship Thee,
>   That echoing in spirit thus
>   One spirit we will be.

> 3 The Father in the Son has come,
>   The Son the Spirit is,
>   That to our spirit God may come.
>   O what a grace is this!

> 4 The Son is Thine eternal Word,
>   The Word is Spirit too;
>   The Spirit as our life has come
>   Our spirit to renew.

> 5 Thy Spirit in our spirit is,
>   And thus in unity
>   Thy Spirit witnesseth with ours
>   That we are born of Thee.

> 6 In everything Thy Spirit leads
>   That we may follow Him;
>   We thus may spiritual become,
>   With life and peace within.

> 7 In spirit we would worship Thee,
>   In spirit Thee address,

Until our spirit is released
Thine image to express.

8 Our Father, we would praise Thee now
That Thou the Spirit art;
In spirit and in truth to Thee
True worship we impart

Mentioning *Spirit* and *spirit* nineteen times, this hymn repeatedly speaks about the relationship between the Holy Spirit and our human spirit. I hope that you will all pay attention to this matter.

THE SPIRIT, THE BREATH, AND THE WIND

The Bible uses three items to symbolize the Spirit—breath, wind, and fire. The two main symbols of the Spirit are breath and wind. Air, or breath, is the basis for the existence of all living creatures. Without air, there can be no living creatures. Because there is no ozone layer around the moon, there is no air around the moon. As a result, no living creatures are able to survive there. If you want to go to the moon, you have to bring air with you. Similar to air, our God is real and experiential as the Spirit. In addition, the Spirit is the basis of the believer's living. Without the Spirit, we cannot survive.

When the movement of air becomes strong, it produces a violent wind. It may even form into a typhoon or tornado. When wind comes, air comes with it. If there is no wind in a room, there will not be enough air in the room, and the room will become stuffy. Hence, wind and air cannot be separated. When the movement of air is strong, it is wind; when wind comes, air comes with it, and once wind is weakened, it becomes simply air again.

The Greek word *pneuma* and the Hebrew word *ruach* both denote breath, wind, and spirit. In the Old Testament the word *ruach* in Ezekiel 37 has these three meanings—wind, breath, and spirit. This word may refer to breath in one verse, to wind in another verse, and to spirit in still another verse. In John 3 the Lord Jesus also used the word *pneuma* with two meanings—the word *Spirit* in the phrase *born of the Spirit* in verse 6 and the word *wind* in the clause *the wind blows where it wills* in verse 8 are both *pneuma* in Greek. How do we know that in verse 8 *pneuma* denotes wind? We know because that which "blows where it wills" is neither spirit nor breath but wind. Thus, to understand the real meaning of a word, sometimes we have to examine its context.

The New Testament says that the Lord is the Spirit (2 Cor. 3:17). We can also say that the Lord is the breath (John 20:22) and that He is also the wind (cf. John 3:8). In the evening of the Lord's resurrection, He came in the midst of the disciples and breathed into them for them to receive the Spirit as their life; that is, He breathed the essential Spirit into them. However, on the day of Pentecost, the Holy Spirit was poured down like a strong, violent wind as the economical Spirit (Acts 2:2). *Hymns,* #212 in the Chinese hymnal says, "The Holy Spirit as a strong wind / Blows from heaven / Upon the congregation, / As He did at Pentecost." In John 20 the Spirit is breath, and in Acts 2 the Spirit is wind.

Today all of our experience of the Lord, of God, and of Christ absolutely depend on the Spirit. In fact, the Lord, God, and Christ are the Spirit. This is what today's Christianity neglects and does not understand. The so-called Modernists do not even acknowledge that the wind and the breath refer to the Spirit. On the contrary, they say that everything is a matter of man's heart and is merely a feeling or a mental reaction. How do you know when the wind comes? You know because you feel it. How do you know there is air in a house? You do not see it or touch it; you feel it. This is the belief of the Modernists. They deny the spiritual reality and the spiritual facts and focus on the mind, which has been corrupted by Satan. They say that both the God who is spoken of in the Bible and the Spirit who is referred to in Christianity are imaginary perceptions. The fact remains, however, that mental perception is based upon feeling, and feeling is based upon something real. For example, you will only sense my love if I do in fact love you, you will only feel pain if I hit you, and you will only feel stuffiness if there is no air in the room. All of these feelings are based upon something real.

The Modernists deny the spiritual reality and talk only about its outward manifestations. They say that zealous

Christians have been captivated by preachers and drawn into the doctrines of regeneration, transformation, and being filled with the Spirit. It may be true that some preachers have the power to captivate believers. But if there were no spiritual facts or reality behind what they preached, how could they have power and how could the believers be captivated? One time a sister testified that she had emptied herself out to the Lord and had thoroughly confessed and prayed. Initially after doing this she did not have any feeling, but an hour later she felt relieved throughout her whole being. The Modernists would say that this was merely a mental reaction. However, would the sister have felt relieved if she had not prayed? Likewise, you feel refreshed after taking a deep breath because there is air all around you. If there were no air, you would not feel refreshed after taking a deep breath. The Modernists also say that the feeling that you have after calling on the Lord is just a mental reaction. However, if you call on other names, do you still have this feeling or this supposed mental reaction? This is something that is worthy of their consideration.

PURSUING TO BE FILLED WITH THE HOLY SPIRIT IN OUR HUMAN SPIRIT

God not only created us with eyes to see, ears to hear, and senses to touch but also with a spirit to contact Him and to perceive spiritual reality. As soon as you breathe, you can sense the fresh air in the room. Similarly, once you exercise your spirit, you can contact and touch the spiritual facts and reality. The key is using the right organ. Hence, Paul said, "'The word is near you, in your mouth and in your heart,' that is, the word of the faith which we proclaim" (Rom. 10:8). This word is the Lord Himself. The Gospel of John says that in the beginning was the Word, that the Word was God (1:1), and that God is Spirit (4:24). The word, which is the Spirit and God, is not far from us; it is in our mouth and in our heart, just like the air. The question is not whether He is there but whether we are willing to receive Him. How do we receive Him? Paul told us the way—"If you confess with your mouth Jesus as Lord and believe in your heart that God has raised

Him from the dead, you will be saved" (Rom. 10:9). As long as we pray, call, and exercise our spirit, we will receive the Holy Spirit.

I hope that you not only understand and focus on this truth but that you also release this truth and pursue the filling of the Holy Spirit. Without deep breathing and fresh air, it is hard for us to be physically healthy. In the same way, without the Spirit and the exercise of the spirit, it is impossible for us to be spiritually healthy and victorious. Thus, you should not merely speak about some spiritual terms, such as *the essential Spirit* and *the economical Spirit;* neither should you simply analyze whether the Spirit is in us essentially or upon us economically; instead, you should pursue to be filled with the Spirit. The people in the region surrounding the lower Yangtze River have a saying—"In the morning the skin encompasses the water; at night the water encompasses the skin." There are not two different waters; it is just that water has two functions. When you drink water, the water is within you, but when you take a bath, you are in the water. This is a picture of mingling. When we are filled with the Holy Spirit inwardly and outwardly, we are mingled with the Holy Spirit. This should be our emphasis today.

LEARNING AND BEING TRAINED IN OUR DAILY LIVING

The burden of this message is to cover some practical matters in your living so that as young people pursuing to serve the Lord, you may receive some practical training and learning in three main categories—eating, clothing, and sleeping and exercise. Sleeping is inactive whereas exercise is active. I am going to teach you something practical about food, clothing, and being inactive and active. Do not think that being active or inactive are small matters. If you are inactive when you should be active, or if you are active when you should be inactive, you will have great problems and much trouble. Therefore, you must be trained in these matters. I thank the Lord that He has kept me on the earth for so long a time. There is a Chinese proverb which says, "Since the ancient times it is rare for human life to reach seventy years." In the Bible Moses said something similar—"The days of our years are seventy years, / Or, if because of strength, eighty years" (Psa. 90:10). I am over eighty years old now, so I am a man with strength. Of course, this is the mercy of God, and I have nothing to boast of. However, you have to realize that the dealings between God and us are always of two sides. For example, suppose that God desires to give us water to drink, but we close our mouth and refuse to drink. If we do this, He cannot do anything about it. Suppose also that God wants to give you longevity, but instead of appreciating His desire to do so, you jump into the sea or run in front of someone's car. If you did this, you would die sooner than others. If this were to happen, it would be because you acted contrary to God's will.

Therefore, from your youth you have to pay attention to your daily living so that you will be healthy and will live longer on the earth. You should not think that since you are young, you are very useful and can be used to do many things. This may cause you to use your body excessively. Of course, you are useful while you are young, but you will be more useful as you become older. No one desires to die early; everyone wants to live longer. I can tell you that the secret to good health depends on eating, resting, and exercising properly. Eating refers to our diet, resting refers mainly to our sleep, and exercise refers to our activities, our bodily exercise.

Eating

When I was young, I did not pay proper attention to my eating. I was always under stress and busy, and sometimes I ate without restraint. Consequently, I developed stomach problems very early in life. Before I reached the age of thirty, I already had a very serious stomach problem. Therefore, you have to be warned. Do not eat under stress, eat in haste, or eat without control. Second, do not pay too much attention to the taste of the food that you eat; rather, pay attention to the nutrition that you receive from it. You should know something about nutrition, and you should also have a little knowledge about such things as oil, sugar, salt, and meat. Third, learn to eat a regular amount—avoid eating too much at times and too little at others. Perhaps in these days you frequently fast. Although this is very good, you should not do it too irregularly. To do so will ruin your stomach. Fourth, as much as possible eat at a regular time. According to your present schedule, I am afraid that you may not eat at regular times. You may either skip supper or eat after the meetings. This is not right. This may be acceptable occasionally, but in the long run you will have stomach problems.

We must know the way our body works. Once a certain part is damaged, it is hard to restore it to the original state and condition. Some of the parts may recover, but it is still not possible to restore them a hundred percent. It is best not to allow anything to damage your body. Do not allow this to happen and then seek to be cured after the damage is already done. The best thing to do is to cherish and maintain your body now. I remind you to pay much attention to the matter of eating.

Resting and Being Active

Regarding resting, you should sleep at night and avoid constantly burning the midnight oil. It is best to sleep early and rise early. Generally speaking, this is the proper way. After lunch you should have at least ten minutes to close your eyes and rest. It is best if you can lie down and take a short nap. However, to nap for more than an hour is excessive.

You should consider exercise and being active as your recreation and leisure, but you must be careful not to fall into sin. It is necessary to be active for the sake of your physical health. Therefore, you should exercise regularly, either doing calisthenics or "shadowboxing" for at least twenty minutes each day. Moreover, it is good to have a little exercise after each meal. There is a Chinese saying—"Walk a hundred steps after every meal; live for ninety and nine years." Doctors, nurses, and all those who are experienced know that eating meals in bed or refraining from any activity after eating is detrimental to one's health. Doctors even encourage the patients who are confined in bed to try to stand up for awhile or to take a little walk after meals if possible.

It is also not good to read or work immediately after eating. The best thing to do after a meal is to walk for three to five minutes, taking around a hundred steps each minute. In this way, you will enjoy longevity. A certain senior statesman in Chinese politics who lived to an advanced age wrote a proverb that contains a formula for longevity. The gist of the proverb is—"To enjoy longevity, you have to sleep seven hours at night and walk seven thousand steps during the day." This man walked one hundred steps a minute, so it took him seventy minutes to walk seven thousand steps. If an elderly man can walk seven thousand steps a day, he will be very healthy, but walking seven thousand steps is not enough for young people. They need more exercise, and it is better for them to have some more vigorous activities. Elderly ones should walk seven thousand steps a day, but it is not too much for children to walk ten thousand steps a day. As young people, you are in between the children and the elderly ones, so you also should have the proper amount of exercise. While you are exercising, however, you have to bear in mind that you are doing so because you love the Lord. I hope that the Lord would grant me another twenty years, because I still have many burdens. The Lord gives us life and breath for us to love Him. This is why we need to be trained from our youth.

Clothing

Clothing is also related to health. In the Bible the main purpose of clothing is for covering. After man's fall, man began to have the sense of shame, and there was the need for him to cover his nakedness with clothing. The first time that the Bible mentions clothing is in Genesis 3. When Adam and Eve fell, they began to have the sense of sin, and they discovered that they were naked. Before man's fall, although man was naked, he did not have the sense of sin. Thus, after the fall, God made them coats of skins to cover their shame. Clothing is also for protecting us from cold. If we do not wear enough clothing, we will catch a cold. In the Bible clothing is mainly for covering, and the more our clothing covers us, the better. The priests in the Old Testament had to have their robes long enough to touch the ground so that others could not see their body. The priests were also forbidden from going up the steps of the altar, lest their nakedness be uncovered (Exo. 20:26).

The purpose of clothing in the Bible is first for covering, and second, for protecting oneself from the cold. Once our shame is covered, we look pleasant before God. However, today people in the world love to expose themselves. Suppose a brother were to come to the meeting in shorts with his calves and knees exposed. If he preached to you wearing shorts, would you be able to receive what he said?

In 1 Timothy Paul says that we should adorn ourselves in proper clothing (2:9). The word *proper* in this verse is hard to define. To dress properly means to dress in a way that does not appear peculiar to other people. My clothing does not look peculiar to others; both older people and younger people feel comfortable with what I am wearing. This is proper. If a brother were to wear a wide tie that had a big cross and the words *In Christ* written on it, how would you feel? Would this not look strange? What about our shoes? If someone were to come to the meeting wearing sandals or slippers and having his toes exposed, and if this one were to stand in front of you to speak, you would surely feel uncomfortable. This is an example of improper dress. If a brother's hair is as long as a sister's hair, and he wears it in a ponytail and puts ornaments in it, this is not sin and is not explicitly forbidden by the Bible, but it is not fitting and is improper.

Paul was wise. He did not go into detail concerning the matter of clothing. He mentioned only that our clothing should be proper. The word *proper* is deep in meaning and broad in definition. Today as you are learning to serve the Lord and to contact people, your clothing should be proper. When you stand up to speak for the Lord, many people will be listening to you and watching you. Thus, you must be careful about your speaking and your behavior, and you must learn how to dress.

Today people pay much attention to fashion and beauty. To them to be beautiful requires exposing their body as much as possible. This is the trend and fashion of the world today. The women's skirts are too short. This is not beauty. This corrupts others' eyes and adds to the women's shame. The more a woman covers her body, the better. This is the reason why there are ancient traditions like head-covering and face-covering. The less the body is exposed, the better it is. It is not only wrong to expose one's bones, flesh, and skin, it is also a shame to expose the shape of one's body with tight clothing. Modern females always try their best to expose not only their skin and flesh but also the shape of their body. They think that this is beauty. Actually, this is to be void of the sense of shame. It is not right for one who serves the Lord to dress like this. If you dress this way, no one will dare to look at you, much less listen to your words.

We should also carefully consider the color of our clothing. Those who serve the Lord should not wear clothes with colors that are too striking or too sharp. It is improper if the color of our clothing is so striking that it draws attention. We should also consider the style of our clothing. If the style of our clothing is too strange, it will make others feel uncomfortable. Even the combination of the colors of our tie and shirt should be fitting. Suppose you wear a navy blue suit with a green tie and a pink shirt. Your skin and flesh may not be exposed, and the style of your suit may be very elegant, but the minute you appear before others, they will be shocked. This is improper.

The colors of your tie and suit should match. They also should not be overly plain, lest they draw unnecessary attention. The colors of your socks should also match the color of your suit. Suppose a brother wears light brown shoes, purple and red socks, and a gray suit with a blue tie. If he were to speak to me, I would not be able to listen to what he was saying because I would be distracted by his shoes, socks, suit, and tie.

God's creation is beautiful, and there is no ugly color anywhere in it. Today while we are working for the Lord, we are constantly contacting people. Therefore, our clothing, which is a form of our expression, should be proper. I am not telling you to have a high standard of living, but I hope that you would pay attention to your status. You were students in the past, and as students you might not have had the means to pay much attention to your clothing. But now that you are working for the Lord and going out to contact people, you should pay attention to the way that you dress, including the style of your clothing, the type of your clothing, and the color of your shoes and socks. If you are careless in the way that you dress, you will compromise your outward expression and depreciate yourself. Today everybody pays attention to outward appearance. Whenever you buy something, you should examine what it looks like before you decide to buy it. I wish that all of you would pay attention to these things and practice and learn faithfully in this matter. All of these things that I have mentioned are part of our character training.

Prayer: Lord, we consecrate ourselves completely and entirely to You. We belong to You, and we are willing to be those who are always filled with You within and transformed by You without. We do not want anyone to despise our youth; instead, we want to be a proper pattern. Lord, have mercy on us and cause us to be aggressive and have much training in all these matters—in eating, in clothing, and in being active and inactive. Lord, adjust us in our character that we may be vessels unto honor, those who are filled with You to express You. Amen.

ABOUT THE AUTHOR

Witness Lee was born in 1905 in northern China and raised in a Christian family. At age 19 he was fully captured for Christ and immediately consecrated himself to preach the gospel for the rest of his life. Early in his service, he met Watchman Nee, a renowned preacher, teacher, and writer. Witness Lee labored together with Watchman Nee under his direction. In 1934 Watchman Nee entrusted Witness Lee with the responsibility for his publication operation, called the Shanghai Gospel Bookroom.

Prior to the Communist takeover in 1949, Witness Lee was sent by Watchman Nee and his other co-workers to Taiwan to insure that the things delivered to them by the Lord would not be lost. Watchman Nee instructed Witness Lee to continue the former's publishing operation abroad as the Taiwan Gospel Bookroom, which has been publicly recognized as the publisher of Watchman Nee's works outside China. Witness Lee's work in Taiwan manifested the Lord's abundant blessing. From a mere 350 believers, newly fled from the mainland, the churches in Taiwan grew to 20,000 in five years.

In 1962 Witness Lee felt led of the Lord to come to the United States, settling in California. During his 35 years of service in the U.S., he ministered in weekly meetings and weekend conferences, delivering several thousand spoken messages. Much of his speaking has since been published as over 400 titles. Many of these have been translated into over fourteen languages. He gave his last public conference in February 1997 at the age of 91.

He leaves behind a prolific presentation of the truth in the Bible. His major work, *Life-study of the Bible,* comprises over 25,000 pages of commentary on every book of the Bible from the perspective of the believers' enjoyment and experience of God's divine life in Christ through the Holy Spirit. Witness Lee was the chief editor of a new translation of the New Testament into Chinese called the Recovery Version and directed the translation of the same into English. The Recovery Version also appears in a number of other languages. He provided an extensive body of footnotes, outlines, and spiritual cross references. A radio broadcast of his messages can be heard on Christian radio stations in the United States. In 1965 Witness Lee founded Living Stream Ministry, a non-profit corporation, located in Anaheim, California, which officially presents his and Watchman Nee's ministry.

Witness Lee's ministry emphasizes the experience of Christ as life and the practical oneness of the believers as the Body of Christ. Stressing the importance of attending to both these matters, he led the churches under his care to grow in Christian life and function. He was unbending in his conviction that God's goal is not narrow sectarianism but the Body of Christ. In time, believers began to meet simply as the church in their localities in response to this conviction. In recent years a number of new churches have been raised up in Russia and in many eastern European countries.